Right Parables, Wrong Perspectives

Right Parables, Wrong Perspectives

A Diverse Reading of Luke's Parables

SAM TSANG

WIPF & STOCK · Eugene, Oregon

RIGHT PARABLES, WRONG PERSPECTIVES
A Diverse Reading of Luke's Parables

Copyright © 2015 Sam Tsang. All rights reserved. Except for brief quotations in critical publications or reviews, no part of this book may be reproduced in any manner without prior written permission from the publisher. Write: Permissions. Wipf and Stock Publishers, 199 W. 8th Ave., Suite 3, Eugene, OR 97401.

Wipf & Stock
An Imprint of Wipf and Stock Publishers
199 W. 8th Ave., Suite 3
Eugene, OR 97401

www.wipfandstock.com

ISBN 13: 978-1-4982-3358-3

Manufactured in the U.S.A.   09/08/2015

Scripture quoted by permission. All scripture quotations, unless otherwise indicated, are taken from the NET Bible® copyright ©1996–2006 by Biblical Studies Press, L.L.C. All rights reserved.

to Anna Scott Bell . . . she knows why.

Contents

Preface | ix
Acknowledgments | xv

Introduction to Reading Luke's Parables | 1
1. Listen and Do? (Luke 6:43–49) | 9
2. Sowing for Results? (Luke 8:1–15) | 17
3. A "Good" Samaritan? Really? (Luke 10:25–37) | 27
4. God the Father, God the Friend? (Luke 11:5–13) | 41
5. Ambiguous Justice? (Luke 12:13–21) | 51
6. Faithful Service and Unfaithful Servants (Luke 12:35–48) | 61
7. The Greatness of Smallness (Luke 13:18–21) | 68
8. Kingdom Faux Pas (Luke 14:7–14) | 76
9. The Impossible Rejection (Luke 14:15–24) | 84
10. The Lost Son? (Luke 15) | 92
11. What's Wrong with Being Rich? (Luke 16:14–31) | 102
12. Kingdom Obligations (Luke 17:7–10) | 112
13. The Unjust/Lazy Judge and Prayer (Luke 18:1–8) | 119
14. "Good" Enough? (Luke 18:9–14) | 126
15. Getting the Most of Your Minas? (Luke 19:11–27) | 134
16. Bad Tenants and the Innocent Son? (Luke 20:9–19) | 143

Preface

WHAT IS THIS BOOK FOR?

JESUS' PARABLES ARE POLYPHONIC. His parables could represent one voice, while there are also multiple voices of ways the stories could have been told. This explains my title and subtitle. The title refers to the wrong perspectives. Jesus was a polemical teacher who didn't hesitate to disclose and denounce the wrong perspectives of his day. The many voices could be the many perspectives people used to view a particular issue, while Jesus emphasized his own perspective. When reading as modern readers, we should keep in mind these perspectives.

There have been a number of very good books on parables in recent years. Klyne Snodgrass's *Stories with Intent* probably provides the most thorough methodological demonstration of various ways to read New Testament parables. Amy-Jill Levine's brief work *Short Stories by Jesus* also provides a uniquely Jewish perspective, demonstrating the provocation Jesus was bringing to his audience while correcting anti-Semitic readings common in the modern West. In this book, I try to be more concise than Snodgrass and focus more on the original readers in addition to Jesus' own audience. My book serves the curious and nontechnical reader who wishes to understand Jesus' parables in Luke.

In this book, I will take sample parables of Jesus in the Gospel according to Luke to show how reading them within their literary and cultural context will challenge both the ancient and modern readers. Inevitably, I shall skip over a few of the parables simply because my purpose isn't to write a thorough commentary on Luke's parables, but to see how a certain way of reading can help us understand any of Luke's parables more

Preface

accurately, creatively, and clearly. At the end of our study, we shall discover that Luke had a very practical and social message that often addresses how resources ought to be used within the faith community and by the faithful individual. It remains a challenging message today in our churches.

I write to serve two primary groups of readers. I serve the busy pastor who wishes to get the gist of Jesus' parables while juggling a busy ministerial schedule. I also serve the lay-person who wishes to go beyond the usual popular studies on Jesus' parables to something with a solid intellectual spine, but without the academic jargon. This effort will cause me to be selective about presenting technical information that may be better suited to academic commentaries on either the parables or on Luke (and there are so many excellent ones out there). My goal is simple. I wish to help my readers appreciate the fact that we often retell Jesus' parables in ways opposite to Jesus' intent. When certain essential elements are missing in our interpretation, we not only risk interpreting a partial truth, but we often derive the opposite message. This book hopes to correct some of our misreading by looking at how ancient audiences could have read them, and then how that also reflects modern misreadings.

This book is also a continuation of my book on Matthew, *Right Kingdom, Wrong Stories*. Readers of *Right Kingdom* will notice similarity in format and differences in content. I will not rehash in detail the preface from *Right Kingdom*. The summary below will serve our purpose in reading Luke's stories.

WHAT IS A PARABLE?

In order to study a parable, it is important to define the term. Scholars have debated what parables essentially are.[1] Are they fables or allegories? Do they have one or multiple points? These questions tend to drive the discussions.[2] Whatever agreements or disagreements, we can't dismiss the fact that these parables had relevance for Jesus' original Jewish audience and Luke's original readers. Thus, their origin was decidedly Jewish but their reception in Luke was Gentile. We shall discuss this matter shortly.

In past discussions regarding parables, many have sought to find a universal model to describe Jesus' parables. Jesus' parables however seem to defy such efforts. While many parables seem to have one clear message,

---

1. For a good discussion, see Snodgrass, *Stories with Intent*, 9–59.
2. For a very simplified discussion, see Tsang, *Right Kingdom*, vii–ix.

Preface

many do not. I think it's probably going to be a tough effort to find that one clear universal model. Perhaps we're asking the wrong questions. Models may or may not determine the meaning. Forms may or may not determine the meaning. So what does?

The interaction between Jesus and his Jewish audience, per the description in the text, determines meaning. Then, the interaction between the author and readers also determines meaning. In other words, every parable encompasses two layers of meaning. How many points a parable makes ultimately doesn't shed enough light to make the debate worth our while. Rather, two boundaries (the interaction between Jesus and his audience and the interaction between Luke and his readers) give us the range of meaning. The parable is the word picture reflecting the issues that are brought up by the two interactions.

WHAT IF PARABLES HAVE IMAGINARY VARIETIES?

In *Right Kingdom*, I asked the question, "What if the parable gets turned upside down?" This is a legitimate question due to the subversive nature of Jesus' parables. Jesus could've told his parables in many different ways, but he chose to tell them in one way. That one way triumphs over the many other ways.

In my colleague Sze-kar Wan's back cover endorsement for *Right Kingdom*, he reminded me that Jesus' parables can be told from "all sides and in all manners." We must recognize that the backward way is not the only way to read a parable. In this study, I shall be more flexible. I ask a slightly different and wider question, "What if parables have imaginary varieties?" What if Jesus endorsed certain mentalities while attacking other mentalities? Whatever Jesus endorsed or attacked would show parts of his teaching that did or didn't fit his society's ideas.

Parables are cultural pieces, or as Amy-Jill Levine suggests, "short stories by Jesus."[3] These are fictional narratives created by Jesus out of the cultural milieu of his day. In other words, Jesus could have told his parables in an alternative way or two, but he chose to tell them the way he did. If we see Jesus' parables as part of a larger cultural conversation, we should also attempt to imagine the other possible ways a parable could have be told, to appreciate its full meaning. Through our imaginative efforts, we can begin to get a glimpse of how value systems that favored or opposed Jesus' value

3. Levine, *Short Stories by Jesus*.

system might implicate our own modern way of looking at life. If we read Luke within the context of each event in Jesus' life, we will find a consistent social message that flows from Luke's understanding of the kingdom and the "gospel."

I hope this book ultimately serves readers from all walks of life, as a part of a spiritual and ethical reflection, which will help shape the way we think and live. All scriptural translations are taken from the New English Translation, just as in *Right Kingdom*. I'm grateful to the NET for granting me permission to use their translation.

METHOD OF READING

In writing this book, I'm not only talking about Luke's message, but also walking through an easily accessible method that both lay readers and preachers can use in their reading. I will consistently follow the following steps to show the possible meanings these fictional stories Jesus told might hold. Through this method, I hope to move the reading from the first-century world to twenty-first-century reality for anyone who seeks their relevance beyond literary entertainment.

To begin with, in the introduction that follows this preface, I will talk about Luke's world and paint a picture of the readership that originally received his message. Certainly, Luke's world was somewhat different from the world of Jesus and his followers. I'll be mindful of the world of Jesus as well when reading the parables. One thing is certain: authors wrote to audiences. As modern readers, we may want to think that the Gospel writers were writing to us. They weren't! They were writing to an ancient audience within certain social conventions. Admittedly, my own experience as an Asian-American Christian with teaching experience in Asia may color my perspective. Such coloring may not be bad because there are some points of convergence between my own culture (or any other culture) and the biblical world. We shall see. In any case, having a background roadmap to navigate these stories from the perspective of the biblical audience is very important for modern understanding. This paradigm will be something that guides our ethical and homiletical reflection at the end of each parable, but we're jumping ahead.

The first step to reading each parable, after we have reconstructed Luke's world, is a reconstructive reading of the parable in an alternate way. In this first step, we look at one way Jesus could've told the parable. In this

Preface

process, we should let the parable speak for itself instead of trying to theologize and moralize it. Quite often, in modern preaching, people do not let the parables speak for themselves but import their own narratives into them. There were obviously many possible ways to understand the parables in Jesus' day. In this study, we'll explore one way as a sample of how the parable could have functioned within its own cultural environment. I shall change what I consider the key element within the parable to see how the parable might have gone in a direction quite different from the intent of the storyteller. The characters of the parable will play an active role in determining how the story would have turned out. Another criterion I use in determining the key narrative element is the overall intent of the parable. In most parables, Jesus talks about what issue or question the parable is trying to address or answer. We can change the key element to address the issue in a different way and see what comes of it. In this step, I will provide my own altered version of the parable. Readers themselves can surely imagine other ways the parable could've been told to address the issue raised by Jesus and his situation.

In the second step, after coming up with an imaginary variation to the parable, I will establish the meaning of each parable as Jesus told it. In so doing, I will address the broader context from which the parable arose. How do I determine where the boundaries are for the broader context? It's quite simple. I use the change of occasion and location in Luke's story to determine the exact event that gives rise to Jesus' parable. After discussion of the meaning of the parable, I will have a subsection called "context" to explore how narrative context influenced the formation of such a parable. This is an important element in determining the initial meaning a parable had for Jesus' original audience. While range of meaning is a relatively open system, this step allows us to attend to what meanings are impossible and therefore narrows our scope. In this second step, we should be attentive to Jesus' background if possible so that we don't read Jesus outside of his own culture.

With the third step, after understanding the parable within Jesus' context in Luke's Gospel, we are ready to jump into more practical discussions. This third step has three phases. First, we discuss what Luke's writing of the story would have meant to the original readers by connecting the meaning of the parable for Jesus' audience with Luke's readers. Second, we look at how the meaning from the original readers transfers to our world by looking at converging points between our culture and theirs. Third, we can look at how knowing all this can impact our preaching and Bible studies.

Preface

The third step will provide some homiletic suggestions for busy preachers and Bible study questions for the busy Bible study leader. Here we'll explore possible misreadings that can be found in the popular teaching of these parables. I'll point out those pitfalls so that we can avoid future mishaps.

These three simple steps will always consider the metanarrative we've reconstructed from Luke's world and they will highlight for us the possible and impossible meanings. This multidimensional reading will end up presenting a Jesus who was socially subversive for his time and ours. Readers will hopefully be able to follow and benefit from this intellectual exercise to further and deepen their personal reflections.

Acknowledgments

No work would be complete without acknowledging all who have contributed to it. I first wish to thank Hong Kong Baptist University (different from my institution, Hong Kong Baptist Theological Seminary) for inviting me to give the Faith in Practice Lectureship in April 2015, where I presented some of the content of this book to three thousand cross-generational listeners for three nights, from young university students in their early twenties to elderlies. I further wish to thank Trinity Theological College of Singapore who invited me to give the Trinity Lectureship in the convocation for the 2014–2015 school year. I had a chance to discuss various homiletic theories in relation to New Testament narratives with their excellent and gracious faculty. The text I have used for this study is taken from the New English Translation (the NET Bible). I wish to thank David Austin of the NET for granting me permission to use their excellent translation. I also wish to thank my family, as always, who put up with my busy traveling and writing schedules in such good humor. They occupy a special place in my heart.

Introduction to Reading Luke's Parables

Luke's World

A TIME OF POLITICAL CHANGES

MANY SCHOLARS DATE THE writing of Luke (both the Gospel and Acts) to after 70 CE. What kind of period was this? At the very least, it was a period of uncertainty with the Roman dynasty changing from one set of monarchs to another. Much of this information can be accessible through Josephus, Suetonius, and Tacitus. Did Luke care about politics? Of course he did because everything happening at the government level would affect the lives of ordinary citizens. As a man of his time, Luke colored his writings with politics, starting as early as Jesus' birth (Luke 2:1) and ending with Paul's trials and incarceration (Acts 21:27—28:31) as well as everywhere in between during Jesus' and Paul's travels (Luke 20:22; Acts 13:7; 16:37; etc.).

Even before Luke's writing of this Gospel, things were looking unstable. In the year 69 CE alone, four emperors competed for the top spot with Vespasian coming out on top. This spelled the end of the Julio-Claudio Dynasty and the beginning of the Flavian Dynasty. While all this was going on, Jerusalem had housed all the anti-Roman rebels that started a war against Rome. Based on what we know about the tension leading up to the Jewish war, anti-Semitism had become a more serious problem in the second half of the first century.

No sooner had the Flavian Dynasty came to power than Rome began flexing its muscles by pacifying Britain. One can hardly blame the Romans for their show of force. They had to use their military might to secure peace. This was no small accomplishment because Claudius had already tried invading and taming the Britons even before the middle of first century. Around the time of the dynastic upheaval, Titus became the emperor. These changes inevitably brought uncertainty to all sorts of people. Thus, the original readers of the Gospel according to Luke were reading in the imperial shadow of Rome. For a person of faith, these changes would prompt reflection. Luke reflected through his stories. Without a doubt, the post-70 CE Roman Empire also deserves reflection in Luke, who includes more political detail and vocabulary in his writings than any other New Testament writer. Just like his hero Paul, Luke would no doubt problematize and reform some of the familiar concepts of his society, especially with regard to how each Christ follower ought to relate first to Jewish society within Roman imperialism and second to the Roman Empire itself.

It is easy to understand the relevance of such political changes because of their parallels in our own time. In a time of political changes, the United States has experienced the surfacing of racial tension, evident in the Ferguson riots and the protests all over the nation, shouting, "Black lives matter!" The widening gap between the rich and the poor now also parallels the ancient social classification. With an election year coming up, many feel lost about where the country is heading. While these and many other issues are complicated, politics and policies will force believers to contemplate what it means to be a Christ follower in this day and age in the same way Luke's narratives confronted his generation.

A SOCIETY OF PATRIARCHAL PATRONAGE

Aside from the political changes in Luke's time, the societal structure during Luke's time remained constant. The law sustaining social order was patriarchal—but the entire Roman social order was patriarchal. Our idea of gender equality simply didn't exist in those days. In such a case, socialpolitics rather than race and gender should be the dominant lens through which we look at literature like Luke's narrative. Gender inequality was only a byproduct of a bigger system. In the empire's history, the governing structure was tyrannical, patriarchal, and oligarchic. Every spring, the Roman state religion declared the beginning of the military campaign season until late fall. At the head of this political machine was the father of all fathers, the emperor himself. He ruled over the nation the way a head of the household (always the oldest surviving male) ruled over his household.

Introduction to Reading Luke's Parables

In such a society, the problem of identity always exists, especially where mixture of identities exists. The duel identity of a Christ follower / Roman citizen whose religious origin was firmly within mainstream Judaism while living in the shadow of the Roman system would baffle many in the readership of Luke's work. A great modern example comes from the French Algerians who are predominantly Muslim living in a secular society with some Christian colorings. What then are such people? Are they more Algerian than French? Is their place of origin or their parents' homeland more important than their adopted country? Would they prefer white French culture or their own ethnic culture? How much of each blends into the others? What about being Muslim? Certainly, the Charlie Hebdo case proves that culture and religion do occasionally and violently clash in a multicultural society, and even an attempt to create a perfect blend of multiculturalism doesn't always solve tension over identity. In the same way, the religious identity of a reader such as Theophilus or of any citizen, like Paul, would have to function within the powerful shadow of the empire while working through the tension in order to stay true to Jesus' messianic movement.

Identity was not always expressed in the form of gender or ethnicity. It also came in terms of social hierarchy. It is common knowledge that the empire was a slave society. That means people with no rights did most of the productive work. As stated above, the head of the political machine was Caesar. He modeled, for better or for worse, the behavior of a head of household. The Romans built their society on the foundation of the household. A household was not a biological/nuclear family in the modern sense. Rather, the household was a social network linked with the head of the household, usually someone immensely wealthy. With the head of household at the top, those who belonged to his household included children, spouse, present and former slaves, and hired staff. Wealth seems to be the distinction, but it wasn't. The main issue was social classification. Rarely could anyone climb that ladder into a middle-class situation. Hierarchy was rigid. People often exchanged favors based on where they fit on the ladder. Relationships, then, were transactional and based on this hierarchy.[1] Rich patrons expected favors, and the poor who lived under them expected protection. This reciprocal relationship is best described as "you rub my back and I'll rub yours." In a hierarchy, there was no free lunch. Free grace wasn't part of the everyday reality of the household. Grace was conditional. At worst, grace became a tool the rich manipulated to get stuff done the

---

1. Tsang, *Right Kingdom*, 3–4.

way someone dangles a carrot in front of a farm animal to get it to move. In such a situation, a person's relationship with another was by nature based on their relative positions within the hierarchy of relationships. Where people fit often determined what they did. Some did veer off to do their own things, but those weren't the customs. No one was completely exempt from the system, even if an occasional variation occurred.

It is easy to see this world as something quite foreign to us, in our time, but it really isn't. Professionally, many are aware of the cliché "It's not what you know but whom you know that matters." Many have flattered their way into higher positions by pleasing the right people and selectively doing tasks that make them look good in their careers. Sometimes, people can't get beyond a certain point in their career because of discrimination or other systemic problems, even in the "free world." In reality, nothing is ever "free." We also have our own hierarchy even in the frees societies in the West. When we go to work everyday, we simply don't get away with disrespecting our bosses continuously while expecting a raise. Even if we hate our bosses, we can't show our disdain day after day without consequences. The major difference for us is that we can get a new job when the opportunities arise, instead of being stuck under a boss whom we despise. Not so the ancient society. People were very much stuck. Without the modern middle class, the rise toward relative freedom from this system was only the stuff of dreams. The higher the person was in the hierarchy, the freer and more powerful that person would be. Thus, the upper tier consisted of very few people, with a majority of the society sitting underneath these people. Obviously, the higher ups of the society still had to answer to Caesar and his ultimate deputies whose jobs were to make sure the system functioned without deviance. Things had to go on like clockwork. In such a patronage society, we can't leave out a discussion about the role of the patron here. This leads to our discussion on Theophilus.

THE BOSS-MAN CONVERT THEOPHILUS

Writing of any kind contains rhetorical conventions conveyed from author to reader/audience. Our starting point ought to be Luke's stated audience. We should devote some space to coming up with a reasonable profile for Luke's readership. The only way to even understand authorial purpose is to first understand the relationship between author and audience. The best place to find this relationship in this Gospel is through the prefaces

Introduction to Reading Luke's Parables

of Luke and Acts. Who is Theophilus, besides being the shadowy figure of Luke 1:1–4 and Acts 1:1? With a name like Theophilus, we can assume that he's a Gentile. Luke explicitly called the recipient Theophilus which means "loved by God." Some may choose to spiritualize this name to mean all who were loved by God, but this name was common enough to see him as the real person *and* Luke's ideal reader. Luke in his Gospel calls him "most excellent" which is a technical term denoting a government official (cf. Acts 24:3; 26:25). Such a title denotes a real reader with a real rank.

Most likely, Theophilus's title describes a person belonging to the equestrian rank (Latin *egregius* or *clarissimus*) or more general magistrate (Latin *optimus*). People like Theophilus belonged to a group from which senators and governors of provinces were drawn (cf. Acts 23:26). These men had to have extraordinary possessions and money in order to keep their ranks. In modern terms, these men owned a fortune that would require several lifetimes to acquire. They were multimillionaires—and that was only the minimum requirement to hold that knightly rank. In today's term, the approximate minimum property holdings for each equestrian rank ought to be something like twelve million US dollars.[2] With globalization, it is easier now than before to imagine that amount of wealth for the super rich, but we still have a middle class. The widening gap between rich and poor doesn't completely eliminate our middle class. Imagine a world with no middle class. That would be Theophilus's world. We find obscene amount of wealth to be extraordinary simply because we have a middle class. We think of the wealth of a multimillionaire as the pinnacle of financial accomplishment today. For Theophilus to hold that rank, it was the minimum requirement. Dipping below the government-stipulated level of wealth would be a huge risk to one's place in the hierarchy, and certainly put the next generation at risk.

Many equestrians received their ranks through their ancestors who had also amassed their wealth dating as far back as the days of Roman Republic. Some got the rank through their loyalty to the Romans in the Republic. By Luke's time, they were more like the wealthy English gentry who lived in relative leisure. With their wealth, they could access the greatest system of power upon promotion. Yet, if we look at the situation realistically, the rich man's job was to amass more wealth, not just for rainy days

---

2. Ferguson, *Backgrounds of Early Christianity*, 53, points out that minimal property holding should be around 100,000 denarii. That's around 100,000 times the average daily wage.

but for sustaining that equestrian privilege for his sons. Amassing wealth, like today, took breeding, financial sense, and connections across generations. If a father's wealth was evenly divided among his sons, the relatively rich children still might not be able to inherit the same privilege of rank. The only way to assure of such privilege was to spawn more wealth through wise investment. An aristocrat like Theophilus had the privilege of getting to the information that could make such benefits happen. Theophilus could further garner more wealth and power by associating with or even dining with the right people. He could also use his underlings to do his bidding to make sure everything would result in gain for him. Being rich was not a part-time job. Relationships were the means to earn greater wealth. To translate this situation into modern English, the privilege of a lifetime comes from our ancestors, but the privilege for our heirs must come from our wise investment. Some of the ways we ensure that our children will land in a privileged situation include making sure they go to the right universities through our own legacy, or get the right internship, or join the right fraternity, and so on. All of a sudden, Theophilus's world was not so far away from our modern world.

Within teachings of Jesus from Luke's perspective, Theophilus could have another option than mere amassment of wealth for his heirs. As a man of some means, Theophilus could choose to sponsor some of the missionary activities of the church. Yet, this would go directly against what he should do for his own welfare. This will become apparent when reading Luke's parables. One way Theophilus could contribute to the church was to open his home for gatherings. Furthermore, his ability to read would automatically put him into leadership, since much of the population at the time was illiterate (a fact especially true among Gentiles). Unless Theophilus and his faith community were still attached to the synagogue, which I highly doubt, there had to be other places where the faith community could meet. With only so few in the Roman society being rich, the only people who had adequate meeting places were the rich. The poor, especially the urban poor, hardly had enough space for their own families. If Theophilus opened his own place for church gathering, then there would be social implications for his own welfare. The later discussions on some of the parables will implicate this aspect, but we'll leave this topic for now. Since Theophilus worked within the imperial patronage system, the social reading of Jesus' parables is a must for modern readers. Luke was not only keenly aware of political history, but he intentionally set God's salvation history into his own social

Introduction to Reading Luke's Parables

context, in the retelling of Jesus' parables, in order to show God's great plan within human history.

What kind of reader was Theophilus? We don't have all the information to answer such a question. The prologue of Luke 1 sounds like a dedication page an ancient writer wrote to patrons. Theophilus must have been some kind of patron to the church or Luke's community. Luke 1:4 also describes Theophilus's spiritual position. Luke 1:4 talks about affirmation that was needed on things that have been taught to Theophilus. History then has meaning beyond facts. They are doctrinal. The truth that had already been taught to him would now be confirmed through the understanding of Luke. In view of Luke's writing style, the book no doubt taught many lessons to Theophilus because it was full of discourses, especially in parable form. These speeches probably weren't verbatim from Jesus' original teaching. Luke shaped them for his purpose to teach Theophilus lessons. Luke meant for Theophilus to hear the speeches to show a summary of the gospel that was preached among the discipleship community. Furthermore, Luke also talked about the handing down of stories and teachings about Jesus through eyewitnesses in Luke 1:1–3. The explicit statement certainly points to the continuation of the Jesus tradition through original eyewitnesses.

When we read Luke with Theophilus's lenses, we need to view the world as the Gentiles did. As it was with any Gentile, Theophilus's original religious orientation would have fit the Greco-Roman profile of polytheism. He would further worship the dead emperors, not necessarily out of religious piety but out of civic duty. What other information can we glean from Luke's writing about Theophilus? Almost certainly, Theophilus had some familiarity with the Jesus tradition (i.e., what the church taught about what Jesus did and said) and Judaism. This is evident by the way Luke liberally quoted the Old Testament. Among all the gospel writers, Luke quoted the least of the Old Testament because his reader was a Gentile. The question remains, however, whether such a Gentile could understand the importance of these Old Testament quotes without first understanding their importance from both the messianic community and from Judaism. If Theophilus the Gentile didn't understand, why did Luke quote at all? Some quotes in Luke were even given without any explanation. Luke simply quoted them as if Theophilus understood.

The most frequent quotes in Luke come from the usual suspects, typical in the New Testament: the Pentateuch, the Psalms, and Isaiah. The clear familiarity with these texts should lead us to conclude that Theophilus had enough background from a synagogue setting to understand these texts. Since people didn't know these texts according to modern verse divisions, Theophilus probably also understood the contexts surrounding the brief quotes. Thus, Theophilus's first contact with the faith most likely came from his experience with the synagogue either as a convert to Judaism or at least as someone who was a friend to the Jews much like the way Cornelius was in Acts 10:1–2, 22. Theophilus was a Gentile who had converted to a kind of Judaism linked to Jesus. His was a true conversion from polytheism to monotheism centered on the worship of one king, Jesus Christ.

In today's terms, Theophilus would fit the profile of someone who had privilege even from birth. He's the man born with the proverbial silver spoon in his mouth. He didn't have a thing to worry about other than securing sound investments. In today's world, he would fly around in his helicopter or private jet once in a while just to make sure all his business ventures are up to par. Most of the time, he has other people doing his bidding. His circle consists of others who are as privileged as he is. They would do the stereotypical activities for rich people, such as hanging about country clubs and golf courses. The poor are basically invisible to him as far as relationships are concerned. The new gospel, however, challenged his entire world. It resisted his familiar world in various radical ways. Even as he lived in his privileged world, the gospel gave him a new identity resulting in a new lifestyle and new action. We shall see in our discussion of each parable how all this plays out and how the gospel challenges such a person to resist certain conventions.

1

Listen and Do?

TELLING IT DIFFERENT: LUKE 6:43-49

> For no good tree bears bad fruit, nor again does a bad tree bear good fruit, for each tree is known by its own fruit. For figs are not gathered from thorns, nor are grapes picked from brambles. The good person out of the good treasury of his heart produces good, and the evil person out of his evil treasury produces evil, for his mouth speaks from what fills his heart.
> Why do you call me "Lord, Lord," and don't do what I tell you?
> Everyone who comes to me and listens to my words and puts them into practice—I will show you what he is like: He is like a man building a house, who dug down deep, and laid the foundation on bedrock. But the person who hears and does not put my words into practice is like a man who built a house on the ground without a foundation.

THE EARLY FOLLOWERS OF Jesus were students. Their religious institutions were an outgrowth of the synagogues, where listening and doing were an important part of their lives. Although illiteracy rate was high in those days (higher among Gentiles), believers would learn by hearing and reciting the teachings read by their literate leaders. After learning for a while, they would internalize the knowledge to apply in real life. Failure to practice would indicate ignorance.

This story Jesus told (as I have arranged it above) is talking about listening and doing. It claims that there are two different kinds of builders. The two-way teaching of Jesus is fairly common. Jesus often talked about making choices that were favorable or unfavorable in relation to kingdom values. Even with this modified version of the story, the moral of the story is very clear. Those who listen should also apply, but what exactly was Jesus saying here by telling his story the way he did?

TELLING IT NORMAL: KEY ELEMENTS IN THE STORY

> 43 For no good tree bears bad fruit, nor again does a bad tree bear good fruit, 44 for each tree is known by its own fruit. For figs are not gathered from thorns, nor are grapes picked from brambles. 45 The good person out of the good treasury of his heart produces good, and the evil person out of his evil treasury produces evil, for his mouth speaks from what fills his heart.
> 46 Why do you call me "Lord, Lord," and don't do what I tell you?
> 47 Everyone who comes to me and listens to my words and puts them into practice—I will show you what he is like: 48 He is like a man building a house, who dug down deep, and laid the foundation on bedrock. When a flood came, the river burst against that house but could not shake it, because it had been well built. 49 But the person who hears and does not put my words into practice is like a man who built a house on the ground without a foundation. When the river burst against that house, it collapsed immediately, and was utterly destroyed!

People with ADD often have other issues associated with the dysfunction. In my case, it's mostly my dyslexia. When I'm tired, it's hard for me to make sense of words, whether spoken or written. For others, they can't stay on course in a single conversation because their minds are racing like a Formula One car around the track moving from scene to scene. Words however are important. Jesus here dealt with words.

The section of Luke 6:43–49 is a conclusion to Jesus' speech (I will discuss the context of Jesus' whole speech at the end of this section). Jesus' speech concluded with two images: the fruit-bearing tree and the parable of the good builders. First, Jesus started with the fruit-bearing tree. He started with the negative stating that no good tree bears bad fruit. The words describing both the good and the bad are interesting. The "good" could describe something with good and healthy appearance, in an agricultural sense. The word "bad" denotes bad quality.

Listen and Do?

After Jesus spoke about the usefulness and health of trees, he began talking about humans. Since humans aren't trees, Jesus used other Greek words for "good" and "evil" in Luke 6:45 that denote moral quality in humans. In other words, Jesus was saying that quality of a human would be analogical to quality of tree and its fruit. Thus, the morally good person who possesses a clear vision would bear fruit that benefits, much like figs and grapes would help the farmer. The morally bad person who possesses a muddled vision (with a deadly plank in his eye) would bear fruit that benefits no one. What then did Jesus consider the source of this goodness or evil? Luke 6:45 says that the quality of the person came from the heart. The language he used to describe the heart resembles that of storage. No reasonable person puts rubbish in his storage. The rubbish belongs in the trash pile. The storage is for beneficial treasures one wishes to keep. Based on the metaphor, one's heart ultimately brings forth good or evil words.

Jesus concluded with a parable of the builder. This parable is a reinforcement of the previous one, especially regarding good work. This conclusion demonstrated to Jesus' disciples that now that they had listened to Jesus, they needed to perform the compatible good work. The problem the builder story wants to address is in Luke 6:46. Many called Jesus "Lord" but didn't do what Jesus said. The word "call" is in the Greek present tense (something different from the English present tense), denoting either a continuous or habitual action. In other words, Jesus was asking, "Why do you keep calling me Lord and do not (as a habit) do what I tell you to do?" The repetition of "hearing" in Luke 6:47 and 6:49 shows the context of the discourse for the disciples. These disciples were hearers, but were they doers? Now, they must perform what they heard.

We must read the saying on two levels. In Jesus' time, before people really recognized his entire status, he was viewed as a respected teacher. The word for "lord" did not have to mean what it means for the church later. Within the story of Jesus in Luke, the repetition of "lord" shows the highest form of respect toward a revered holy man who could also perform miracles. For Jesus' disciples, the saying could mean something like "Why do you keep on claiming that I'm your most revered mentor and not do what I tell you?" The logical incompatibility between the claim and the action is the point of the saying. For the churchly reader however, the saying would grow into a true understanding of all that Jesus meant to the church. Thus, readers should obey even more and not less, knowing all that they knew about Jesus in retrospect.

Right Parables, Wrong Perspectives

A careful reader will notice that in the modified telling of the story at the beginning of this chapter, I took out the storm that hit the houses. It is important to note that the missing storm makes what Jesus said somewhat less harsh. So what if people heard but didn't do? There were no consequences (i.e., no storm). At worst, their laziness just made them bad people. However, there were consequences. The emphasis shouldn't be taken away from the consequences. When a person did what Jesus taught, he would be like a man who has built deep foundation and remains unshakeable in the face of the storm-induced flood (Luke 6:48). Commentators interpret this storm in various ways, from divine judgment to the general storms of life. Within the close context of Luke 6:22–23, 26, 28, the storm seems to be persecution from enemies. What then happens if a disciple does not live by Jesus' principles? He would be like a man who did not build a house on proper ground. Building a house on bad ground would be an amateurish mistake. Especially in denser cities, the people would build and cluster together. The chance of building on bad ground would be fairly low because people watched for where others built and then would build close to those areas. Thus, Jesus was talking about a near impossible situation unless it happened in a rural farming community. The well-learned disciple wouldn't make such a mistake but maybe some did. If built on bad ground, the house would not be able to stand when storm water washed away its foundation (Luke 6:49). Thus, when dealing with a tough season, a person who followed Jesus' principles would be able to withstand the persecution or opposition that would come (Luke 6:22).

What exactly did Jesus teach or what did they hear? For the answer, we need a broader understanding of what Jesus just taught within the event of the story. Let me summarize. In Luke 6:20–26, Jesus talked about disciples being aware of their place in the world as the persecuted "others." In Luke 6:27–36, Jesus talked about how disciples were to react to oppression: with love and generosity. In Luke 6:37–42, Jesus talked about disciples as those who would be accurate and fair in judging while making sure they did not commit the same error. These are the basic teachings of Jesus, and he expected all those who called him Lord to follow them with love, generosity, fairness, and integrity.

While the fruit bearing metaphor speaks primarily of good work, the builder story extends further to the stormy part of living on this earth as disciples. Jesus was not contrasting a believer with an unbeliever. He was talking to his disciples. The builder story is in some ways more severe than the fruit tree metaphor because safety and lives are at stake with buildings. Safe buildings provide shelter. Shoddy buildings create liability and even death. Somewhere, some disciples will build their houses on the bad foundation of inconsistent lives, while claiming Jesus to be Lord. As they ignore his teachings, they will be like the builder who built a house on a bad foundation. The house will fall on the builder and destroy his life when hardship and persecution come.

While fruit bearing focuses on good judgment and good works, the good builder parable focuses on good works as a foundation of faith. Many who are from the Protestant Reformed tradition may find this troubling because Luke seems to be going against Paul's theology of justification by free grace. This is not a description of a full soteriology. It is talking about the corporate body of the kingdom containing individual disciples who called Jesus "Lord." Those calling Jesus Lord will build their faith on putting Jesus' teachings into practice. We mustn't read our theological concerns into Luke's. It was natural in that society for people to obey whomever they called "lord." Jesus' words here are very much based on that system. Lordship implies thorough obedience. Lip service had never been enough when it came to "lordship" in Jesus' society. Neither will it suffice for a vibrant faith today.

CONTEXT

Let's now look at the meaning of the images, especially the parable in context. Once more, the transition word at the head of the sentence in Greek is "for," connecting the present discussion to what Jesus taught within the event of Luke 6:17–42. Jesus talked about the eye in Luke 6:41–42 in connection with the fruit bearing metaphor. In other words, good fruit comes from good vision. Why did Jesus want his disciples to judge properly? A self-righteous person is too blind to be a good teacher who bears good fruit. The good vision necessary for bearing good fruit is also essential to good judgment. Thus, the tree is compatible with the fruit it bears. The key, though, is having clear vision. Jesus then illustrated with different kinds of fruits what he meant by "good fruit." He talked about fruits that could be eaten in Luke 6:44, figs and grapes. Neither figs nor grapes could be picked from thorns and briers. Thorns and briers were bad trees. They were of no value because they produced nothing for human consumption.

Within context, the logic of the whole teaching of the tree goes something like this. The "for" at the head of Luke 6:43 should cause us to connect between the teachings of Luke 6:43–45 with Luke 6:41–42. This reconstruction creates a clear message. Vision comes from an accurate self-evaluation. Such a clear vision is important so that when words come out, they will be like good fruits being beneficial to the recipient. In other words, the disciples' words reflect the inner quality they possess.

When reading these teachings, it is easy to get casual with them. Not being able to listen well is certainly a problem, but the problem lessens when there are no consequences. However, if one's very life or death depends on listening, the problem of hearing and practice becomes much more serious. That really is what Jesus (or Luke) was saying. Listening but not doing has its price and the price is deadly. Jesus' warning was stern. The text still speaks sternly now.

PUTTING THE TEXT IN HISTORY: MEANINGS FOR THE WORLD OF AUTHOR-READERS

The teaching of Jesus prepared the disciples not merely for lives of integrity. He was doing much more. He was teaching the disciples to deal with oppression. Jesus also taught about creating a community that should be circumspective and, more importantly, introspective in its judgment. The care members ought to take comes in the area of attitudes, words, and deeds.

For Theophilus, he was the default patron of the community. His literacy, privilege, and natural leadership would have allowed him to shape the attitude, words, and deeds of the community. As the head of this community, Theophilus would have recognized that the ultimate "lord" was Jesus Christ. In our free societies where individual rights are respected, we most likely don't understand the word "lord" the same way as both the ancient author and reader. In Theophilus's time, with the changing of Roman dynasties, the political flux demanded that he would choose the right master to ensure his own prosperity and political success. To call someone "lord" was to submit one's life in its entirety. Yet, Luke used a lordship story to inform Theophilus about who the ultimate lord was, so that every decision he made in these uncertain times would reflect that relationship.

In terms of words, we ought to understand the way ancients viewed words. Jesus talked about the listening and practicing of his words. Leaders of his community would pass Jesus' words down from generation to generation. Not only would they pass them down; they also had to put into practice these words. Just like when Jesus talked about leadership and teaching just prior in Luke 6:39–40, so Luke's parable taught Theophilus about leadership and teaching. One special feature of the early Christ community was its continuation of the teaching tradition from the synagogue. Theophilus would eventually transmit Luke's writing along with other traditions he received about Jesus. In those days, not everyone could use words to influence. Only the privileged and educated could do that because rhetorical training was only available to the most educated. Theophilus was among the privileged. When talking about words, we aren't just talking about a literal faithfulness in passing down words of Jesus. We're talking about using one's privileged position to do the work of the kingdom. Jesus' demand was precise. Words only meant something when they were modeled for recipients of the Christ community. Privilege was the means by which a person served that community. For someone like Theophilus, to call Jesus "lord" would by itself completely turn his world upside down, but for Luke, this was only the beginning. The words and deeds had to match for Theophilus to be a true disciple.

The context surrounding the discourse is oppression or persecution. The moral of Jesus' teaching is quite simple. He wasn't merely talking about listening and doing. He was talking about developing a strong community life in the habit of listening and doing, so much so that when persecution would come, nothing would shake and fall down.

MODERN IMPLICATIONS

The present teaching by Jesus implicates the modern faith community. Recent news tells us that one former Christian band member quit Christianity altogether and declared himself an atheist. While we can't judge his faith journey, his reason for quitting was due to the fact that the organized Christian religion has such stringent rules that mask struggles. He has a point here. Jesus prefaced the present teaching with a discussion about accurate judgment that makes allowance for the judge to be wrong. The wrong judgment that hasn't been born of correct vision will inevitably lead to a community built on ground without foundation. When hard times come, such a community will crumble. Indeed, many segments of organized Christianity have fallen on hard times. Even though many churches are getting bigger, the number of Christians hasn't really increased in many parts of the

West. Many Christians think that the problem is secularization. Perhaps they're half right, but quite often, the church needs to look at what Jesus said. Poor judgment would destroy the community. If the church has been living in ignorance and apathy during easy times, then when hard times come, she will crumble. Jesus' teaching speaks to today's church because the church has suffered bad PR for quite a while by selective morality without a broader and more comprehensive obedience.

One of the mistakes preachers and Bible study leaders make is to see the set of teachings as merely about listening and doing. When it's all about doing what Jesus said, the preacher dooms Jesus to the role of a moralistic sage and nothing more. Another mistake some preachers make is to harmonize the present set of sayings with Matthew 7:15-27. While it is possible to see crossover meanings from the two passages, Luke's teaching differs in emphasis. Matthew was talking in general term in the concluding lines of Jesus' Sermon on the Mount. Luke's story is more specifically about the urgent oppression in the troublesome near future. In some ways, Jesus' words point to a future when hard times would come. When hard times come, the church could crumble, not because of the hard times but because she had not created a culture or lifestyle of understanding and obedience to Christ. Thus, instead of blaming the hard times the church can't control, the blame should be placed on the church culture. The greatest enemy is internal. If a preacher wants to tackle this text, one good way is to put the storm at the end in the same way Jesus did it so that the emphasis is not so much the *what*, but the *why* of obedience.

REFLECTION QUESTIONS

1. How does the elimination of the storm change the parable?
2. What is the emphasis if the storm is included in our reading?
3. Why isn't this just a story about listening and doing?
4. What other examples of failure do you see in our churches in recent times?

2

Sowing for Results?

TELLING IT DIFFERENT: LUKE 8:1-15

> A sower went out to sow his seed. He then plowed the ground before sowing to ensure that the seeds all fell into the right places. He further plowed yet once more to make sure the seeds get turned over into the soil. At the end, he received a great crop.
>
> Now the parable means this: The seed is the word of God. Whoever sowed the word is the sower. Since the sower wanted maximum results, much preparation needed to take place. The end result was a great harvest. Preparation is everything.

I TELL THE STORY differently based on farming practices in Jesus' day. The reason why the story ought to have been told this way is simple. In Luke's day (as in Jesus' day), food production was a very important issue. We have records of riots over food in the Roman Empire. Farmers were important contributors to such a society. The sower in the story was probably a tenant farmer who lived on a piece of land while working for the landlord. His job was to make sure that he didn't waste seeds and maximize profit for his boss. This would ensure that he would remain in good standing with his boss. Wasting seeds would dishonor his boss.

Today's farming is no different, as humans have invented many machines to help make planting easier and more profitable. If we want results, we need to plow, and plowing was a regular practice in Jesus' day (e.g., Luke 9:62; 17:7). The story told above is about adequate preparation so that whatever word was sown would produce the desired results. This alternate story has a very modern, utilitarian feel to it. If we want to maximize gain, minimize pain, and create the greatest profit, that is how we should farm. Jesus told it differently, but what exactly was Jesus saying here by telling his story the way he did?

TELLING IT NORMAL: KEY ELEMENTS IN THE STORY

1 Some time afterward he went on through towns and villages, preaching and proclaiming the good news of the kingdom of God. The twelve were with him, 2 and also some women who had been healed of evil spirits and disabilities: Mary (called Magdalene), from whom seven demons had gone out, 3 and Joanna the wife of Cuza (Herod's household manager), Susanna, and many others who provided for them out of their own resources.

4 While a large crowd was gathering and people were coming to Jesus from one town after another, he spoke to them in a parable: 5 "A sower went out to sow his seed. And as he sowed, some fell along the path and was trampled on, and the wild birds devoured it. 6 Other seed fell on rock, and when it came up, it withered because it had no moisture. 7 Other seed fell among the thorns, and they grew up with it and choked it. 8 But other seed fell on good soil and grew, and it produced a hundred times as much grain." As he said this, he called out, "The one who has ears to hear had better listen!"

9 Then his disciples asked him what this parable meant. 10 He said, "You have been given the opportunity to know the secrets of the kingdom of God, but for others they are in parables, so that *although they see they may not see, and although they hear they may not understand.*

11 "Now the parable means this: The seed is the word of God. 12 Those along the path are the ones who have heard; then the devil comes and takes away the word from their hearts, so that they may not believe and be saved. 13 Those on the rock are the ones who receive the word with joy when they hear it, but they have no root. They believe for a while, but in a time of testing fall away. 14 As for the seed that fell among thorns, these are the ones who hear, but as they go on their way they are choked by the worries and riches and pleasures of life, and their fruit does not mature. 15 But as for the seed that landed on good soil, these are the ones who, after hearing the word, cling to it with an honest and good heart, and bear fruit with steadfast endurance."

Sowing for Results?

This story is critical to the Synoptic Gospels. Because it's the most elaborate parable in Mark (4:1–20), many interpreters think that it gives an interpretive paradigm for the entire Gospel of Mark. This story also occupies a large portion of Matthew 13.[1] As we shall see, within Lukan literary and historical context, this story meant something different. Here's a great example of the same event in Jesus' life creating different meanings for different gospel authors and their audiences.

It is a simple parable. The farmer's goal was obvious. He wanted to get as fruitful a harvest as possible. The strangest thing was the way the man scattered seeds. The usual way to deal with the ground was to till it (cf. Luke 9:62). Plowing was a typical farming practice, whether in a Jewish or non-Jewish context. At least, breaking up the soil would guarantee a better harvest than to randomly scatter seeds. Maybe someone may want to guess that the tilling came after the random sowing in Jesus' parable, but the parable doesn't mention a subsequent tilling. The final bearing of the fruits shows that there wasn't any subsequent tilling. My alternate version of the parable above is the normal way of breaking up the soil before sowing.

Even if the farmer planned to plow, then Jesus' story is a picture of someone carrying a bag of seeds over his shoulder, with an undiscovered hole that was leaking seeds all over the ground as he went out to plow good soil. The good soil at the end of the parable is obviously the destination he had planned to go, where the soil was already prepared and plowed. Jesus used the singular "seed," as is common in parables. Its singularity fits what Jesus wanted to say, because Jesus was talking about the singular word of God.

Four kinds of surfaces receive the seed. Let me summarize. First, in Luke 8:5, the path did not receive the seed well as people trampled on it and birds ate it up. It's shocking that multiple birds ate one singular seed. Second, in Luke 8:6, the rock did not receive the seed well because it withered from having no moisture. Third, in Luke 8:7, the thorns choked out the plants coming from the seed. Fourth, in Luke 8:8, the good soil grew a good plant, yielding one hundred times the amount. Jesus finished in Luke 8:8b by encouraging everyone to listen to this parable. The irony is, without explanation, probably no one understood Jesus. The parable was strange in so many ways, from its plotline to its impact on the audience.

Did Jesus mean for his listeners to understand the parable? Jesus called the parable "knowledge of the secrets of God's kingdom" in Luke 8:10a. The "secrets" are in plural in the Greek. This shows that the parable has multiple

---

1. For my take on Matthew 13:2–23, see Tsang, *Right Kingdom*, 11–21.

lessons both related to Isaiah 6:9 and the context of Jesus' (and possibly even in the disciples') ministry. Jesus quoted Isaiah 6:9 in Luke 8:10 when he answered the disciples' inquiry about the meaning. Jesus was analogizing the lack of understanding of this parable to the exiles who were doomed to fail in their faith. Jesus' context was a large crowd that was gathering in Luke 8:4. Jesus basically said that most of them, apart from the disciples, had no idea about the parable or anything else Jesus taught. They were to face failure and judgment.

It is easy to over-interpret and say that in all times, the majority will also misunderstand what Jesus teaches. This may or may not be the case, but at least we can say that most of Jesus' audience was in the dark. More important is that Jesus wanted to give four different scenarios, in which only one scenario bore fruit. The Isaianic quote seems to contradict Luke 8:8b. Most likely, Luke 8:8b shows the accessibility of Jesus' teaching to anyone who had an ear. Yet, hearing didn't equal understanding, though. Luke 8:10 shows that even with access, understanding Jesus' teachings was quite another matter. Thus, even accessibility didn't equal understanding. The parable certainly functions to veil rather than reveal, as the quotation of Isaiah 6:9 suggests.

Now, Jesus explained the parable in Luke 8:11-15. Through the seed, Jesus was talking about the word of God, presumably words he spoke because the quotation of Isaiah clearly indicates YHWH to be speaking, but Jesus spoke in the parable. We may not read too much Christology into the narrative, but surely such a statement has implications about the identity of Jesus. Jesus' explanation was completely consistent with his Isaiah 6:9 quote in Luke 8:10. The parable not only explained its own meaning, but also clarified what Jesus' quotation means. Jesus was talking about the numerous reasons why the word was not received. First, in Luke 8:12, Jesus pointed out that the devil kept people from hearing. Second, in Luke 8:13, Jesus pointed out that rootlessness kept them from retaining the word. Third, in Luke 8:14, worries, riches, and pleasure choked out the word to keep people from maturing. Fourth, in Luke 8:15, noble and good-hearted helped people to hear and retain the word while persevering through hardship to bear permanent fruit.

When looking at the climax of this parable, the fruit bearing was a hundred times more than what was sown in Luke 8:8. Moreover, Jesus talked about the heart as good and noble. Common to all the soils in the entire plotline is the hearing of the word. They all heard in Luke 8:11-15, but the ideal result was to retain, persevere, and bear fruit. In Luke 8:15, the mention of clinging to the word means that these fruit bearers did not only hear, but they made the word their own. By mentioning this, Jesus was not talking about an easy life. Instead, the pressures the other three soils had to face surely played havoc on the good and noble heart as well. Surely, the devil, the fleeting rootlessness, the worries, riches, and pleasures put immense pressure on the kind of people with good hearts just as much as the others. While trying to bear fruit, they had to overcome such pressures and persevere.

The parable has not yet ended. Jesus provided further elaboration in Luke 8:16–18 that coheres well with his Isaiah quotation in Luke 8:10 and with the parable. In Luke 8:16–17, Jesus basically talked about the public function of the light. Most likely, the light parable is an analogy to the crop of Luke 8:15. A crop, like a light, has to be seen. For a lamp to be put under any cover is foolish. So it is for a plant that does not bear fruit. The manner of hearing then becomes the central issue in Luke 8:18. Jesus was addressing his disciples here. The disciples were to listen in a manner that would bring forth a public expression of the word. Jesus' last word stated that whoever had would be given more and whoever does not, whatever he thinks he might have would be taken away also. Who exactly was Jesus referring to? Probably Jesus was referring to all who heard the message in the prophecy of Isaiah 6:9 in Luke 8:10. Those who thought they had were probably those who heard Jesus without holding on to what was taught and bearing a crop. Out of all four kinds of people, only one would bear a crop. The parable itself is the partial embodiment of Isaiah 6:9. The good soil was the only part that did not fit Isaiah 6:9.

It is important to note before we draw conclusions that Jesus was not merely talking about individuals. Surely, he was talking about individuals, but he was also talking about the kind of people who had the seed sown on them. Many factors had contributed to the barren situation, but whatever the factor was, Jesus took good work seriously. Hearing of God's word should create good work. Listening is ultimately the focal point due to the fact that so many people were surrounding Jesus. The danger according to Luke 8:18 is that some might have thought that they had heard and understood, even though they never had.

Right Parables, Wrong Perspectives

CONTEXT

To appreciate this story, we must read it from its real beginning where the event triggered Jesus' parable. The location for this story was in some town and the occasion was the teaching before a crowd of people (Luke 8:4). Before talking about the parable, Luke inserted a list of women in Luke 8:1–3 to explain how Jesus was able to afford the expense of traveling from place to place without having to work. This will remain an important detail when we revisit the conclusion of the story. Overall, the staging of the story has much to do with ministry expenses.

The story itself also has its own problem statement. The setting shows that many people were coming to Jesus in Luke 8:4. The gathering crowd in Luke 8:4 shows the increase in number of people as a steady stream. This steady stream of people gave Jesus the impetus to describe the scene using a parable. Thus, within the story, the parable is not "about us" but about the scene Jesus was facing.

Luke's writing of this meaningful parable points to the few people who actually did anything for Jesus. The women in Luke 8:2–3 typify the kind of fruit bearing Jesus was looking for, while the rest of the crowd that didn't understand in Luke 8:4 probably typifies the other three soils that didn't bear fruit. The narrative makes sense typologically because there's no other way to explain why Luke needed to insert this list of women in an otherwise complete parable. Certainly, even without the women, the typology of the parable makes sense. With the few women in stark contrast with the large crowd however, the parable makes even more sense.

What about the concluding point? The conclusion is actually Luke 8:16–18. Jesus had an ethical admonition for his disciples in the guise of a short parable. Jesus ended with a warning for those who listened (i.e., the disciples) in Luke 8:18. I didn't deal with Luke 8:16–18 as a separate parable because it continues from the soil parable without a break. We should perhaps look at the lamp story as an illustration or analogy of the parable of the soils. It is important to note that the discussion about lighting a lamp and putting it on the stand rather than hiding it is quite relevant to the soil parable. A lamp functions to give light in a place where everyone can see. In the same way, the soil is meant to bear a crop. This discussion about listening is then putting the soil parable into the context of discipleship. The manner of listening should result in bearing fruit or a crop. Jesus never completely dismissed that the disciples could be the fruitless soil. That's why he warned them to be careful about how they listened. The other three types of fruitless soil presented not only real danger to the crowd, but also served as a warning to the disciples. With this concluding remark, Jesus was saying that the disciples ought to produce good works, much like the women did, so that they could demonstrate that they were the good soil and the light. These women were doing their part, and now Jesus implored the disciples to do theirs. The story is a perfectly told narrative about discipleship, not merely a tale about good soil versus bad soil.

PUTTING THE TEXT IN HISTORY: MEANINGS FOR THE WORLD OF AUTHOR-READERS

Women's place in society was much lower then men's in Luke's world. Theophilus was at the opposite end of the spectrum from the typical woman. He was the head of household. As a great patron of the faith community, Luke was teaching him that gender hierarchy in no way affects one's place in the kingdom. In fact, Luke singled out these women by matching them with Jesus' parables to make them role models. In Theophilus's society of honor and shame, Luke was greatly exhorting Theophilus to rise up to the level of these women by being fruitful. If these women who were in lowly positions and had fewer resources could do it, Theophilus, a man of great means, could do even more.

What might prevent Theophilus from rising to the challenge? The three types of soil illustrated for him the challenges he had to face. He had to be aware of all sorts of distractions and become intentional in his way of discipleship. Discipleship within the parable and within Theophilus's community came from the word. Theophilus's faith community, much like the average faith community, was a community centered on the word. In the case of Theophilus, what he had were the teachings of Jesus, Luke, and the Old Testament. When practicing his piety, he would hear or even teach some of these materials. Before the transmission could happen, he had to internalize and practice. The reason Jesus gave was clear. He had to firm up everything before the great storm of life would hit him. In Theophilus's time, the uncertainty of the Roman dynasties and the political storms could easily challenge his social prosperity. He could prepare not so much by amassing more material goods, but by bearing a good crop. His work would ensure his longevity as a kingdom citizen.

MODERN IMPLICATIONS

The sower parable is equally challenging for the modern Christian. Globalization has caused many new challenges. One of the challenges is the job market; our job security is as vulnerable as ever. Imported workers who will (sometimes) work for less with greater competencies create certain tensions in our lives. Modern Christians may think that amassing more wealth is the solution. In fact, many modern churches do just that. When the income of the churches depends on how the job market impacts the congregants, money becomes a big issue. Jesus knew that.

Money can be a distraction in bearing fruits because it either brings worries in bad times or pleasure in good times. The advancement of electronic media also presents yet another challenge that may stumble many in their faith. Many electronic gadgets make sounds and send notices when a message or update comes. Just imagine how many times we check messages today versus twenty years ago and then we'll appreciate the challenge modern technology presents. With our lives being governed by every update, it is easy not to reflect on the deeper things and be like the shallow soils. Rootless Christianity is quite evident everywhere. People read or reflect less and less. Many church leaders think that the solution is to get the latest electronic technology, and that technology will solve the ultimate problem. Jesus said the opposite.

Riches and technological advancement aren't bad. They're necessary in some cases, but when they occupy the faith community in the form of bigger and fancier facilities or facades, they distract from the real issue. When hard times come, neither money nor technology will save us. In fact, a church can be the most fancy of them all, but fail to be a church at all. All that is left would be a beautiful shell with its high tech equipment. Churches then become theaters of hollow dreams.

Jesus' solution is the same for the modern church when it comes to the essence of its community. The community, large or small, has one duty. Its duty is to listen, reflect, and finally practice the sound teaching of God's word. That seems to be the focus all along. The community's good work will ensure that no matter what life situation hits, it will survive.

This parable is full of pitfalls. One pitfall preachers may experience is the harmonization of this parable with Matthew 13:2–23 and Mark 4:1–20. In Matthew, the parable pretty much has a mission emphasis. Matthew's readers were diaspora Jews who struggled with the kind of real-life situation in which they found themselves. Mark's record seems to use this as an interpretive paradigm to characterize all those who would listen to Jesus in Mark. Some have failed, but others had succeeded at different times. The disciples even failed at times. The situation of sowing perfectly illustrates such a mixed bag of reception in Mark. Now with Luke's story, the sowing parable illustrates something about the result of sowing in terms of good works. Luke's story shows a clearer ethical concreteness than Matthew or Mark. Luke's story isn't merely descriptive; it is directive. The modern sermon must also have a directive tone if the preacher wants to tackle Luke's version.

When pastors preach from this passage, it is easy to get bogged down with the idea that minority of the soil is Christian. That's celebrating a kind of sectarian victimhood. Christianity is by default the religion of the West. Calling Christians a minority in the West amounts to a big joke. Some preachers may say that some aren't "real" Christians, as if they themselves know what a real Christian is. These aren't exactly the best ways to approach the text. Jesus wasn't too explicit about the good soil being a minority. In the narrative, the women *were* the minority, but that only applies to their time. It is wrong to apply the text as if that's the case even now. It's equally problematic to read the text as if there are really four different types of soils. In reality, there are only two types of soils (i.e., the fruitless and the fruitful) with three different types of problems. The three different types of problems create one type of soil, the fruitless soil.

We must focus on several issues in our preaching on this passage. First, we should focus on the point that the ability to see, hear, and understand come entirely from God. This reliance on God comes from the Isaiah 6 quotation in Luke 8:10. Humans by their own volition can't understand the word of God, according to what Jesus just said. Second, we should focus on the reality that many factors keep people from understanding besides divine initiative. Jesus didn't resolve the problem of God's election and human free will here. He just left it. Third, most importantly, the fruitful soil can be found in the most unexpected people, like these women. Apparently, any kind of people can become good soil. A strategy of preaching this section should be to focus on the parable itself and then leave the surprise at the end that the women were the real fruit bearers.

REFLECTION QUESTIONS

1. How does the elimination of the women change the soil parable?
2. What role does Isaiah 6 play in the parable?
3. If you were to compare this narrative with Matthew 13:2–23 and Mark 4:1–20, how would you describe the differences between the points these authors were trying to make?
4. What theological tension didn't Jesus resolve?
5. What was the purpose of the parable?
6. What was the role of women in that society?
7. How does the parable speak to the modern church?

3

A "Good" Samaritan? Really?

TELLING IT DIFFERENT: LUKE 10:25-37

> A man was going down from Jerusalem to Jericho, and fell into the hands of robbers, who stripped him, beat him up, and went off, leaving him half dead. Now by chance a Samaritan was going down that road, but when he saw the injured man he passed by on the other side. A Levite, when he came up to the place and saw him, he stopped to look. And a priest who was traveling came to where the injured man was, and when he saw him, he felt compassion for him. Together, both men went up to him and bandaged his wounds, pouring oil and wine on them. Then they put him on one of the animals, brought him to an inn, and took care of him. The next day they took out two silver coins and gave them to the innkeeper, saying, "Take care of him, and whatever else you spend, we will repay you when we come back this way."

To those who have attended church Sunday school for some time, the animosity between the Samaritans and the Jews is probably nothing new. In fact, the verses in Luke 9:52–53 also indicate the very same fact. A comparable situation today would be something akin to the conflicts between Jews and Palestinians. When the northern kingdom of Israel was captured by the Assyrians and had transplanted people to live in the northern kingdom (2 Kings 17:24–41), the Samaritans were the result of this event. Intermarriage between some of the remaining Israelites and foreigners from where the Samaritan emerged probably took place at that time. While this group certainly adopted some Gentile practices, it most likely tried to follow the Torah as well because the Samaritans had their own version of Scripture that was very similar to the Jews'. The biggest problem was not race but religion and politics.

During the period between the two Testaments, the Samaritans didn't side with the Jews but instead sided with the Gentiles. Space doesn't permit me to go into any detail on this aspect. The most important thing to remember is that the Samaritans and Jews weren't good friends. The animosity continued in Jesus' day.

With all that in mind, the above retelling of the story would have made more sense to the average first-century Jew. Imagine a man coming from Jerusalem. The text doesn't say that he was a Jew, but we may safely assume his Jewish identity based on the direction of his travel. The two religious workers, though slightly different in their roles, certainly would have helped out a fellow Jew. They would have recognized his plight and ethnicity. As such, they were obligated to help him. He was their brother. Since they're both moving away from the temple precinct, they were both "getting off work." Why would they not help? The Samaritan, however, seeing the same situation, would have had a much different reaction.

Although we can't take away the compassion and humanity of the Samaritan, he would have been the least likely of all the passerby candidates to help the poor man. When he actually helped the victim, he was not a "good" Samaritan. No! He was a "bad" Samaritan according to his culture. One question remains, "Were the religious leaders good Jews?" Jesus told the story so differently, but what exactly was Jesus saying here?

TELLING IT NORMAL: KEY ELEMENTS IN THE STORY

> 25 Now an expert in religious law stood up to test Jesus, saying, "Teacher, what must I do to inherit eternal life?" 26 He said to him, "What is written in the law? How do you understand it?" 27 The expert answered, *"Love the Lord your God with all your heart, with all your soul, with all your strength, and with all your mind,* and *love your neighbor as yourself."* 28 Jesus said to him, "You have answered correctly; do this, and you will live."
>
> 29 But the expert, wanting to justify himself, said to Jesus, "And who is my neighbor?" 30 Jesus replied, "A man was going down from Jerusalem to Jericho, and fell into the hands of robbers, who stripped him, beat him up, and went off, leaving him half dead. 31 Now by chance a priest was going down that road, but when he saw the injured man he passed by on the other side. 32 So

A "Good" Samaritan? Really?

too a Levite, when he came up to the place and saw him, passed by on the other side. 33 But a Samaritan who was traveling came to where the injured man was, and when he saw him, he felt compassion for him. 34 He went up to him and bandaged his wounds, pouring oil and wine on them. Then he put him on his own animal, brought him to an inn, and took care of him. 35 The next day he took out two silver coins and gave them to the innkeeper, saying, 'Take care of him, and whatever else you spend, I will repay you when I come back this way.' 36 Which of these three do you think became a neighbor to the man who fell into the hands of the robbers?" 37 The expert in religious law said, "The one who showed mercy to him." So Jesus said to him, "Go and do the same."

The story sounds familiar to anyone who has attended church for any length of time. It is a most beloved story with a character that has become part of our own cultural vocabulary, the Good Samaritan. The question remains, "What's so good about the Samaritan?" Before we dive into the context of the story, let me suggest several angles from which the story can be read.

First, we must look at it from the geographical angle because that's the way the story started. Very likely, Jesus got his inspiration from his trip up to the Jerusalem via his Samaritan location (beginning in Luke 9:51). This geographical move toward Jesus' final mission caused Jesus to lay out before the lawyer the value system Jesus represented. The traveling direction of the man is downward in Luke 10:30 toward Jericho from Jerusalem mainly because Jerusalem sat on a plateau. The road moving away from Jerusalem had a very steep drop. The robbers, laying in wait below, pounced on the unaware victim because that road was treacherous with many places to hide. The downward sightline made it hard to detect an ambush, and the victim's downhill travel would make a backward retreat impossible. The priest and Levite also went down the same road in Luke 10:31–32. The direction was the same between the two religious men and the victim. Both the priest and Levite were potential victims of such a robbery as well. The actual victim was just unlucky.

Some popular interpreters talk about how helping the victim would have rendered both the priest and Levite unclean if the victim died and they touched the dead body. Whether the dead body would render either man unclean is still debatable. A more important point is that neither man needed to be ritually clean to perform their professional duties because they were not moving toward Jerusalem. They were getting off work, so to speak. They were already done with their duties.

In contrast, Jesus' description of the Samaritan was ambiguous regarding his traveling direction in Luke 10:33. The Samaritan was just traveling somewhere. There's no geographical convenience or inconvenience about the way Jesus described his travel. Jesus told the story in this geographical fashion to highlight the calloused attitude of the religious leaders here. Jesus also told this story to highlight his own mission. The reason why Jesus went to Jerusalem in the first place was because the Jerusalem religious institution (i.e., the priest and Levite in the story) had failed. Jesus had to accomplish what the Jerusalem religion could not accomplish.

Second, we can look at the story ethnically. While making distinction between the Jewish leaders and the Samaritans (as we've already discussed above), Jesus didn't give the ethnic identity of the victim. We can safely assume that he was a Jew but such an assumption only comes from seeing him in terms of his traveling direction. Jesus left the man's ethnic identity simply implied, but unstated, to point out that ethnic/national identity was secondary to his being a victim. Misfortune could strike both Jews and Gentiles alike, and good deeds came out of the least expected people. Victimhood is universal. The law expert's answer to Jesus' question also speaks volumes. Instead of stating that the Samaritan was a good neighbor, he merely spoke of the person as the one who had mercy on the victim in Luke 10:37. The law expert simply couldn't fathom the story. Neither could he bring himself to speak of the ethnic identity of the Samaritan. The answer, though tainted with ethnic tension, also negated the victim's ethnicity. Either way, Jesus told him to go and do likewise. In other words, if a despised Samaritan whom the law expert didn't consider lovable or orthodox could do this, how much more an expert of the law of Israel should do it? Based on the ethnic tension, Jesus didn't lay out the maximum application of mercy and neighborly love. He was teaching the basic meaning and application.

Third, we can read the story rhetorically. Jesus made a rich rhetorical move by using high-ranking religious leaders in his parable to answer a law expert's inquiry. In a very focused manner, Jesus' parable was a polemic against the law expert's institution. The interesting storytelling of Jesus repeats the word for "seeing" in Luke 10:31–33. All three characters saw, but what they did with the vision shows the kind of people they were. Since the law expert asked about the minimal good deed he could do to justify himself, Jesus showed through the parable that collectively those in the religious institution hadn't even fulfilled the most minimal duty. The parable became a portrait of failure for the religious institution of Jesus' day. The irony is that the Samaritan fulfilled the Law where the religious leaders failed. In some ways, the parable was a mockery. While the religious leaders failed to even fulfill the minimum, the Samaritan fulfilled to the maximum in his follow-up care for the victim in Luke 10:35. The contrast then was also between zero effort and max effort. While the law expert wanted to fulfill minimally, Jesus asked for the maximum. His goal of justifying himself in Luke 10:29 also remained unreached.

CONTEXT

The context of the parable isn't often discussed with any detail, but the parable is full of great interpretive possibilities. The traditionally touching story of the Samaritan should receive new understanding based on its role in the overall narrative of Luke. It's even a misnomer to call the Samaritan a "good" Samaritan because Jesus didn't explicitly call him good. Perhaps it's better to label him the "merciful" Samaritan.

Before we can discuss further the implications of the Samaritan story, another issue deserves some attention. Some may choose to see the Samaritan as Jesus. Was the story symbolizing Jesus' journey being like that of the Samaritan's? We can't be sure. The law expert surely wouldn't have understood the Christological symbolism. It is probably too much to read Jesus into the Samaritan's action. Furthermore, many fail to appreciate the fact that Jesus was not directly answering the questions of the expert in the law but in reality was answering his question in a roundabout way.

Now, we need to focus on the question of the law expert that triggered Jesus' parable. The idea of inheritance within the question "what must I do to inherit eternal life" shows that the law expert thought that eternal life was something waiting for him. Inheritance only went to those who were heirs. The law expert asked the question in light of God's promise to Abraham's heirs. Many people wonder why Jesus even brought up the ethnic dimension. The idea of eternal life within Judaism provides the clue. The law expert could have been siding with the Pharisees who thought that there would be resurrection of the righteous at the end. More important than all this is the way promises and faith functioned in the first century. While there might have been exceptions, the common bond between all Jews was the promise of God. Every Jew was born into the promise by default. There was no need to convert or have a personal experience with God. They had a covenantal relationship with God. This relationship is why Jesus focused on the ethnic aspect in the parable.

The location of the parable is unclear, but surely it is part of the trip toward Jerusalem as stated in Luke 9:51. The occasion is a legal test from an expert of the law in Luke 10:25. The issue is simple: "What must I do to inherit eternal life?" The expert called Jesus a "teacher," a label with a mixed message. It was even applied to John the Baptist in Luke 3:12. The word "to test" also describes the devil's temptation in Luke 4:12. This rhetorical description indicates sinister intentions perhaps to obtain damaging information in order to accuse Jesus of some kind of false teaching. The nature of the question is intriguing because it indicates that in the mind of the questioner, there were many different ways to inherit eternal life. When reading such a question, it is easy to read it in terms of the modern popular idea of "getting saved." Before we come up with an entire set of modern theological propositions, we must first retreat back to the first-century Jewish background to appropriately understand what such a question meant to Jesus and his listeners.

The question Jesus asked in Luke 10:26 contains two parts, "What is written in the law? How do you understand it?" Both the content and interpretation of the law are important. The man then quoted a verse that would have been part of every Jew's lifestyle in Luke 10:27. It comes from Deuteronomy 6:5. This law was part of the "Shema" that begins in Deuteronomy 6:4. In those days, people did not have chapters and verses. Most likely, many Jews memorized large parts of the Torah since their childhood. This quote deals with their relationship with God and relationship with neighbors, thus making the two inseparable expressions of one's faith.

Jesus agreed with the man's quote in Luke 10:28. He told him to practice the quote so he that would live. The idea of living was expressed in the future tense, showing the man's potential to inherit eternal life. Yet, the man now had a different motivation besides testing Jesus. He wanted to justify himself. The way Luke used the word "justify" and related words (cf. Luke 18:9) is decidedly negative in describing those who belonged to the scribal and religious party (cf. Luke 16:15; 18:9). The law expert obviously spoke as one who was already "in" the covenant community, as he was not only born a Jew but studied and taught God's word. He was not trying to justify himself in order to be "saved" in modern evangelical terms. He just wanted to appear righteous as the qualified interlocutor of Jesus' teaching. In Luke, such religious leaders had a kind of pseudo-righteousness that was not righteous in comparison to those who were truly repentant (Luke 18:14). The primary reason for this thread of narrative is that the man dwelled on his ability rather than his inability to fulfill the law. The law expert was trying to justify his own position within the overall faith community to ensure that he too would receive the blessing in the last days of God's judgment. Here, the person was looking for minimal fulfillment by putting a limit on the definition of neighbor. He asked, "And who is my neighbor?" The question could be read as "Who is my neighbor so that I can fulfill the law?" or "Who is my neighbor so that I can tell you that I've already fulfilled my duty?" Jesus gave the answer through the parable.

The clever rhetorical move Jesus made in response to the question "Who is my neighbor?" needs our attention because most commentators do not dwell adequately on this question. It is one of the important questions within this dialogue, and was the primary question that triggered the parable. We must now go back to that question. Most commentators get the idea that Jesus wanted the man to be a good neighbor, and they would be right, but they don't often think about Jesus wanting to answer "Who is my neighbor." Usually, the interpretation is the simple "Don't ask who your neighbor is, but be a neighbor to others."

Contrary to the popular readings, Jesus did not abandon the law expert's question at all. The parable contains the answer. The story shows clearly that the Samaritan was the neighbor to the victim, while the priest and Levite both walked by—perhaps because they were afraid to be the victims, for the story shows that anyone could be a victim. The Samaritan saw the same scene and knew that anyone could be a victim, thus causing him to have compassion in lending a helping hand. While the Samaritan is clearly the neighbor, only the victim knew that the Samaritan was the neighbor. The victim also knew that the religious leaders weren't his neighbors. The victim experienced the answer to the law expert's question only after being stripped of all that he had, including his ethnic identity. To put the answer to the question another way, the victim experienced neighborly benevolence only in dire circumstances. Only the victim could identify the neighbor in the parable. Perhaps in this answer, Jesus was telling the self-justifying law expert to strip himself of his self-sufficiency.

Jesus' parable then serves as a double-edged sword, pointing out on the one hand that being a good neighbor to others is important but on the other that empathy with the victim was equally important. Only through identifying with the victim can one realize who one's neighbor is, even in a surprising person (i.e., a hated Samaritan). Only when people are stripped of everything can they understand who the real neighbor is. The law expert (and the religious leaders in the parable) had a lot, so much so that the law expert felt that he was qualified to justify himself (in light of the knowledge displayed in Luke 10:27–28, and his social rank). The question the law expert asked was theoretical. Instead of focusing on the theoretical nature of "Who is my neighbor?" the answer Jesus gave was practical. Jesus' practical answer can be summarized by the following sentence: "Unless you've been victimized, you'll never know who the real neighbor is. When you suffer, anyone can be your neighbor, even a despised and surprising Samaritan. Sometimes, you also need to identify with the helplessness of the victim in order to identify your neighbor. Meanwhile, be a neighbor to others." The parable is deep in that Jesus addressed the very attitude of the law expert in testing Jesus. The logic in summary looks something like this:

Problem: Who is my neighbor?

The Samaritan	The Victim
My Neighbor	Me?
The Neighbor needing to be identified	The Law Expert

Conclusion: The Samaritan is to the victim as the neighbor is to the law expert. Since the Samaritan was the neighbor, the law expert had to identify himself with the victim. Only then would he be able to identify other neighbors in the way the Samaritan did.

Jesus addressed both the attitude and inquiry of the law expert using the parable. Right from the start of this account, the law expert thought that he was qualified to judge Jesus, but in asking the law expert to identify with the victim, Jesus showed the law expert to be helpless, much like the victim of the robbery. His neighbor might even appear to be the least likely candidate, his imaginary enemy the Samaritan, but his arrogance would keep him from seeing the possibility. Unless he realized that he could have been as helpless as the victim, he would not be able to identify his neighbor and do good to him. Neither could he justify himself or his own action.

A "Good" Samaritan? Really?

Now that we have noted Jesus' two-pronged conclusion of being a neighbor and empathizing with the victim, we should look at the narrator's conclusion about Martha and Mary in Luke 10:38–42. The problem with many interpreters on this story about Martha and Mary is the failure to appreciate its placement here as part of Jesus' journey to Jerusalem right after the parable. It is easier to keep the story of the Good Samaritan separated from the story about Martha and Mary, but Luke had framed them together as part of the same narrative of the same time period until there is a chronological switch in Luke 11:1. Based on our present method of using location and occasion to wrap up one event, Luke leaves us no choice but to read the two stories together as one because both occur about the same time, as Jesus traveled to Jerusalem. If we were to read the stories as one, then where does the Martha and Mary story fit? I believe the story of Martha and Mary is the extended conclusion to the Samaritan story, and the story of the Samaritan fits well with the Martha and Mary story.

While the Samaritan story shows a certain ethic via Jesus' parable, the Martha and Mary story is the narrator's way of providing a point of view about what one must do to inherit eternal life. One should never miss the fact that Jesus was talking about all this on the way to his own death. Although the conclusion of the Samaritan story has to do with good deeds, the Martha and Mary story provides a more complete conclusion. Thus, I see the Martha and Mary story as a part of a second conclusion to the bigger question the law expert asked about what kind of good work one must do to inherit eternal life.

We must note that this second conclusion of Luke in this event focuses not on Mary but on Martha. Quite often, we make Mary the role model which is partially right because Jesus said that she had chosen the better. However, the narrative devotes an overwhelming amount of material to Martha while Mary kept quiet. Thus, the primary interpretive issue should be the question "What's the problem with Martha?" rather than "What's so great about Mary?"

Without a doubt, "preparations," the word for "service" from which the English word "deacon" originates, was a positive description in the original Christian community (e.g., Acts 6:2, 4). All kinds of services in the early church were commendable, not just washing dishes or taking care of meals. By nature, Martha's work was good for Jesus, as much as other early church services were good for that community. If we read the story in light of women's roles in the Roman household, we should gain a somewhat different perspective. There was nothing inherently bad about what Martha did because she received Jesus with hospitality as a friend of the kingdom, like other friends of the kingdom (cf. Luke 9:4; 10:8, 10). While the narrator talks about Martha being distracted, Martha herself accused Mary of leaving her to do all the work. Her problem was her attitude. As a result of her attitude, she was distracted. What she did was not bad, but Mary had done better. The social good Martha did could become better if she would stop being distracted.

Further reading of this scene in terms of Greco-Roman customs would shed more light as well. Within Luke, the symbolic lordship of the position at the feet suggests positional hierarchy (cf. Luke 7:36–50). More than likely, Mary acted as a guest while treating Jesus as the honored host or the lord. There is no need to even debate whether Jesus' lordship was the focal point. It certainly was the focus, as evidenced by the repetition of the word "lord" throughout the chapter. The irony is in the way Martha addressed Jesus as lord while simultaneously telling Jesus what to do in Luke 10:40b. By the emphatic repetition "Martha, Martha" in Luke 10:41, Jesus was clearly frustrated with Martha's suggestion. Thus, this is not a story about contemplation and meditation being better than active service, as some may be tempted to suggest. Mary's action implicated issues beyond her role modeling. She pointed to the messianic mission that would ultimately prioritize the words of the messiah (symbolized by Mary's action) over traditional societal conventions (symbolized by Martha's action). She also taught a lesson about not being distracted by any kind of service, though service was no less important. In the story of the two sisters, the female role is the means by which Jesus taught a lesson for both men and women.

This important story follows the conversation with the law expert. The two stories make a perfect pair because both stories define what good works are at the end. But Jesus did even more. Jesus broke boundaries by talking about both the Samaritan and Mary positively. As important as it is that Martha's story is socially revolutionary in terms of gender roles, Jesus' messiahship is the point that should not be missed. At the same time, Martha also provides a good connection with the Samaritan. Both did good work with one difference: Jesus approved completely the Samaritan's work while he met Martha's good work with relative disapproval. In other words, the Martha story curbed the intensity of the Samaritan's story with a balance of attitude with hard work. In so doing, Luke used a story about women not just so that he could teach about women's roles, but more importantly to teach lessons about attitude for the church, beyond gender stereotypes. Hospitality must be done with a good attitude. This story extends well into the choosing of the seventy-two as well. When we look at what Jesus did here, he had been Lord throughout the choosing of the seventy-two, the debate with the law expert, and the final commendation of Mary.

Thus, when we read the two stories, the Samaritan and Martha/Mary stories, the whole message is greater than the sum of the parts. Four messages come out of my macroscopic reading. First, both deal with Jesus as the lordly interpreter of the law and the social convention. Jesus is Lord! The Samaritan story ended with Jesus giving a command while the Martha and Mary story was open-ended but also inevitably imperatival. Much like the Samaritan story, Jesus was also saying to Martha, in so many words, to go and do likewise, but the conclusion is so obvious that Luke left the ending a bit more open-ended. No one should forget that Jesus is Lord. Second, the good work of the Samaritan came from his empathy while the good work of Mary came from the recognition of Jesus as Lord. Empathy and Jesus' lordship need to go hand in hand. Third, the unusual characters of the Samaritan and Mary show that good work can be found in the most unexpected places. Conventional wisdom can only go so far when defining good works. Jesus taught his followers to look for surprises even while living within social customs. Fourth, both the stories of the Samaritan and of Martha emphasize the right attitude. The Samaritan showed compassion and mercy. Martha lacked the right attitude. Good aren't enough if the attitude isn't right.

PUTTING THE TEXT IN HISTORY: MEANINGS FOR THE WORLD OF AUTHOR-READERS

For Theophilus, these stories surely provided some ethnical foundation for how to live within the imperial system that favored power, status, and hard work. The stories suggested to Theophilus how to be a proper disciple by aligning his life with the proper priorities of showing mercy toward those who were downtrodden and submitting to the authority of Christ. The lessons wouldn't have been easy; Jesus' story turned all the imperial values upside down. Instead of making those with good status great, Theophilus encountered the surprise of Jesus' story, as the lowly and despised Samaritan was shown to be the hero.

For Theophilus, the story of the Samaritan must have seemed quite strange. In his system, Rome vanquished all its enemies. In his own political ambitions, surely he would not have tolerated enemies who might endanger his career. Yet, the messianic neighborliness anticipates even the enemy to be a potential neighbor, thus creating the empathetic potential to forgive them. Who is my neighbor? Quite possibly my enemy! Luke especially dismissed ethnocentricity as one of his core values by hiding the obviously Jewish status of the victim. Luke worked backward by bringing out the Samaritan's ethnic identity at the end.

Through these stories, Theophilus would learn that sometimes being focused on status is not the right way to live. Even though he occupied a high social status, he must imitate the unimaginable Samaritan and also identify with the victim. By reading and obeying the teaching, Theophilus would have to bring himself down a few notches. The call for humility also points to the Martha story. Jesus' teaching points out Martha's multitasking to remind Theophilus that the top priority might not always be hard work or merit. The lordship of Jesus was the basis for setting priorities. By seeing himself as helpless like the victim in the Samaritan story, Theophilus could see Jesus as his ultimate power source. Lordship only comes when one sees one's own helplessness. Discipleship rises out of helplessness.

MODERN IMPLICATIONS

Sympathy comes from empathy. Before empathy can come, however, divisive labels have to be put aside. All this takes courage to put prejudices aside. The parable teaches some modern ethics about what righteousness actually means. It goes beyond name-calling or score keeping. It goes to the realistic issue of helping victims of violence or some other kinds of abuse. It also goes to empathizing with victims no matter which side the victims happen to be on. The politics of Jesus' kingdom are about making a difference that goes beyond mere exegetical precision, social activism, or prophetic denouncements (though all three are important). It is about seeing the suffering of the world and doing something about that suffering by being a neighbor to the victims. The vision all three men in the parable saw points to the need to respond. What we do with what we see determines whether we're indeed doing what we ought to inherit eternal life (i.e., living life as the people of God). However, we mustn't forget that first, we're also often quite helpless ourselves. The lordship of Jesus really demands that disciples

A "Good" Samaritan? Really?

confess they don't have all the abilities or answers, or even whatever it takes to live out that inheritance of eternal life. Self-righteousness (moral righteousness or theological righteousness) is nothing but filthy rags when put before Jesus' standards. Only when we realize that we should identify with the victim rather than the victor can we bend down to see where "the other" (the Samaritan) can possibly contribute to our edification.

The parable is also quite relevant in terms of how we can be good Samaritans. The basis for our good work is empathy, realizing that we too could have needed a neighbor because we too could have been victims. Jesus answered the law expert by putting the victim as the one receiving the firsthand experience of neighborly love. In the same way, the church should actively seek to empathize with those who suffer. In the history of modern evangelicalism, the church does not always speak out on behalf of those who suffer. The excuse is that we just need to "preach the gospel." Literally countless pastors use that mantra of only preaching the gospel and nothing else, especially when they plant a mission while siding with an oppressive regime. Such a callous posture is the exact opposite of Jesus' message. Such preaching is ironically anti-gospel because it doesn't practice grace or justice. When we arrive in any place, God grants us the vision so that we can do justice. When suffering is all around, we can't help but see unless we're physically and spiritually blind. To make matters much worse, many churches also fall into the Martha problem, that of running ahead with annoyance and enthusiasm, without pausing for a second to think about Jesus' lordship. In essence, the modern evangelical church (in general) lacks both the empathy and the mercy of the Samaritan but has accumulated much of the trouble of Martha.

The stories we just read certainly will give any preacher a big challenge. It is difficult to nail down the double question regarding eternal life and the identity of the neighbor Jesus was attempting to answer in the parable. I think the traditional question that tends to drive the preaching of the Samaritan parable is "What must I do to inherit eternal life?" Preachers won't go far wrong if they conclude with Jesus' simple answer: "Be a neighbor." Yet, the surprise of the parable should land on "Who is my neighbor?" The logical complication of answering that question points to the necessity of being identified with the victim to get the answer. The preacher must conclude finally that before one can be a neighbor, one has to gain sympathy through empathy.

With the limited time of modern-day church services, there won't be time to deal with the complicated relationship between the Samaritan parable and the Martha story. It's best however to remind ourselves that understanding the Samaritan story in light of the Martha story makes a difference in the way we preach the Samaritan story. Martha's story is about serving with a focus on Jesus' lordship. If this is the relationship with the Samaritan story, then the preacher will realize how necessary it is to bring empathy into the church culture. When we preach the Samaritan story, we should allow for a little more time to conclude with the teaching on empathy, since it is a complicated concept. In general, when a concept has not been commonly taught in churches, preachers should allow some extra time for digestion.

REFLECTION QUESTIONS

1. How did Jesus answer the two questions?
2. What happens when we retell the story in a different way?
3. Who are some ironic modern equivalents to the "good" Samaritan?
4. How does the Martha and Mary story connect with the Samaritan story?
5. In what way are these stories relevant to the church?

4

God the Father, God the Friend?

TELLING IT DIFFERENT: LUKE 11:5-13

> Suppose one of you has a friend, and you go to him at midnight and say to him, "Friend, lend me three loaves of bread, because a friend of mine has stopped here while on a journey, and I have nothing to set before him." Then he will reply from inside, "Do not bother me. The door is already shut, and my children and I are in bed. I cannot get up and give you anything."

THIS IS A STORY about annoyance. No one wants to be bothered in the middle of the night, especially in Jesus' time. These days, it is easier to imagine being generous simply because we have electricity. We have the choice of not going to sleep too early. In Jesus' time, this was not so.

In those days, streets were not as well lit as today. Oil lamps and candles lit houses. Naturally, in an agrarian society, people had to sleep early because they had to get up early to go about their business or farming. In some parts of the world, this pattern still holds true. With so little lighting, once a person goes to bed, all activities cease. In fact, if one were to get up in the middle of the night to do anything, it would have been extremely troublesome. Entertaining a friend in need would require one to get up, light a lamp and then look for the stuff the friend needed. Today, such an undertaking would be annoying. In those days, the degree of annoyance multiplied.

Many who read this story would take it for granted that the hospitality Jesus talked about was commonplace. I'm not too sure because Jesus did say that this was an audacious (and even rude) move to knock on the door not for one's own need but for a need of a friend of a friend. Obligation diminished quickly. More importantly, middle of the night was not suppertime. The request was most unreasonable. The most reasonable response was to tell the friend to go way, but Jesus didn't tell the story in that way. What exactly was Jesus saying here by telling his story the way he did?

TELLING IT NORMAL: KEY ELEMENTS IN THE STORY

> 1 Now Jesus was praying in a certain place. When he stopped, one of his disciples said to him, "Lord, teach us to pray, just as John taught his disciples." 2 So he said to them, "When you pray, say:
> Father, may your name be honored; may your kingdom come.
> 3 Give us each day our daily bread,
> 4 and forgive us our sins, for we also forgive everyone who sins against us. And do not lead us into temptation."
> 5 Then he said to them, "Suppose one of you has a friend, and you go to him at midnight and say to him, 'Friend, lend me three loaves of bread, 6 because a friend of mine has stopped here while on a journey, and I have nothing to set before him.' 7 Then he will reply from inside, 'Do not bother me. The door is already shut, and my children and I are in bed. I cannot get up and give you anything.' 8 I tell you, even though the man inside will not get up and give him anything because he is his friend, yet because of the first man's sheer persistence he will get up and give him whatever he needs.
> 9 "So I tell you: Ask, and it will be given to you; seek, and you will find; knock, and the door will be opened for you. 10 For everyone who asks receives, and the one who seeks finds, and to the one who knocks, the door will be opened. 11 What father among you, if your son asks for a fish, will give him a snake instead of a fish? 12 Or if he asks for an egg, will give him a scorpion? 13 If you then, although you are evil, know how to give good gifts to your children, how much more will the heavenly Father give the Holy Spirit to those who ask him!"

The parable in Luke 11:5–13 comes after a teaching about prayer. We shall discuss its relationship with prayer later. The common understanding is to view the story as a transaction between two parties. People popularly understand the saying to mean something like "a friend in need is a friend indeed" where a needy friend directly asks for bread. The story instead looks something more like this: A friend came in from far away unexpectedly.

Upon finding out about the presence of the unexpected friend, the disciple went to the neighbor and asked for food for his friend simply because the disciple's house had run out of food. The sincerity of the man who asked was evident in the word he uses for lending in Luke 11:5. The word can mean something like an interest-free loan. Was the man serious about getting a loan? This is a question we can't answer. We can't help but gasp at his audacity in using the word for a loan. The Greek word describing this entire request in Luke 11:8 actually means something like "shameless." Was he going to pay his friend back, just for bread? This seems crazy but considering the fact that bread machines had not been invented, making a loaf of bread from scratch might have been a hassle. In a society of honor and shame, only the closest friend would dare to be this shameless. The shamelessness was due to the fact of an already existing friendship within a certain code of honor. This friendship allowed the man to break the code of politeness. No wonder the person with food was annoyed in Luke 11:7. In other words, this is a story about relationship and obligation, but as we shall see, it teaches much more.

CONTEXT

The disciples were listening to Jesus' prayer in Luke 11:1a because the passage said that when Jesus finished, they talked to Jesus in Luke 11:1b–2. We must notice that in Luke 11:1, the disciples asked Jesus to teach them to pray in the way "John taught his disciples." The motive behind why they asked Jesus was because John also taught his disciples. The discussion didn't say what John taught his disciples. Certainly, John taught them to pray also, but perhaps the sentence implies more than teaching them how to pray or just teaching them to pray. In Luke 3, we have samples of John's teaching. His teaching was remedial to the problems of his society. He first started with their identity as Abraham's children in Luke 3:7–9 and their failure to fulfill that identity. Then, he talked about the reparation of relationship and repentance for sins in Luke 3:10–14. His teaching ministry along with his prophetic call caused the people to think of John as the Christ. Apparently, the expectation of the messiah was that he would teach. Jesus then fulfilled the disciples' expectations here by addressing some of the same issues and beyond. Jesus then concluded the story with his own teaching in Luke 11:2–13.

We start with the "Lord's Prayer." Technically, it is not really the "Lord's" prayer. It is the disciples' prayer, evident in the corporate language of "us" throughout. The phrase "He said to them" in Luke 11:2, 5 breaks the passage in half. Yet, these parts are related within the Lord's Prayer. The addressee is the Father in Luke 11:2. Jesus' direct address to the Father in Luke 10:21–22 was now mirrored by the disciples' address to the Father. There are a lot of arguments these days about whether God should be addressed with such a patriarchal term. The arguments from both sides miss the point that the biblical God was neither male nor female. The Father was not his name. This was a metaphor for God from a patriarchal society to convey an idea. Furthermore, within the Roman society, this father figure with authority resembled the head of the Roman household. In this case, God the Father became head over the disciples who had established the new household, eventually consisting of slaves and free. The prayer also demonstrates the mission of the church, especially when visiting unbelievers would come to observe the gathering (much like the proselytes of the synagogue). By the confession of God's people about God's supremacy, the nations would know that YHWH was much greater than any other god. This will shed light when it comes to the parable because the parable was about the character of a true friend. At the level of the Lord's Prayer, it was really about the character of God. Thus, just as the authoritative God the Father answered prayers, the true friend helped his friend in need.

The fatherly address of the prayer draws from both the authority and the care a father has for his children. The parable doesn't provide just a comparison; it provides a contrast. While a very best friend would get bread for his friend's friend, the father's care for his children, especially when the children make a request, would far surpass the best friend's friendship. The needs in the prayer include material supply (Luke 11:3), healthy relationships (Luke 11:4), spiritual strength (Luke 11:5), and finally and most importantly a strong future in the Spirit (Luke 11:13).

There's yet another connection between the word "bread" in the Lord's Prayer and the parable of the friend. In Luke 11:3, Jesus taught the disciples to ask for their bread, implying that God would supply the bread. Although the friendship parable here points to a greater reality of God's care, we have to say that the parable illustrates how bread was to be shared among really good friends. The good friends shared with each other and also with a friend's friend because of the God-centered and prayer-centered community they lived in. Prayer then affected how these friends treated each other

God the Father, God the Friend?

in a significant way. So their treatment of each other launched the more meaningful discussion about God's provision by Jesus here.

Now that we've derived the meaning about prayer from the fatherhood of God in the teaching of the Lord's Prayer, it is also important to look at the concluding remarks after the friend parable in the second part of Jesus' teaching (i.e., Luke 11:9–13). The division point is "so I tell you" in Luke 11:9, which indicates the switching of topic. This second part is important in that it progresses from a human parable to the character of God. We must be careful to note the limitations in the comparison that the friendship parable offers. If Jesus' disciples were to compare the friend to God, God would be greater both in generosity and care. God is much more than just a friend. So, we mustn't equate the friend with God. If we make an exact equivalence, then God would sound more like a grouchy and hesitant helper rather than the generous father. Essentially, Jesus was arguing from smaller (i.e., friendship) to greater (i.e., relationship with God). If a human would help a shameless friend because of a relationship, how much more would God help a good Jew who prayed to him in an earnest and pious manner? As we note the difference between God and a human friend, we may ask the question of why people would need to make requests such as Luke 11:3, if God already knows all of our needs. The relationship illustrated in these stories shows that the reason to ask is because it's part of maintaining and demonstrating a healthy relationship. Persistence in prayer only shows a belief in a good God who cares for his children. The question of why people need to pray to an all-knowing God will be further answered in detail in Luke 11:5–13.

The answer starts with a misunderstood passage about "ask, seek, knock" in Luke 11:9. It is a mistake to define each term and ask questions like "What is he trying to ask? What is lost that he has to seek? Did he find and finally see that it's a door? Why is he knocking instead of walking through the open door?" and so on. The point is that these actions show a sincere and even intensifying attitude of prayer, progressing from asking, to seeking, to knocking. A sincere person persists. Also, Luke 11:5–8 seems to point to persistence as being a key factor. Jesus wanted to make sure to address it. Would persistence be enough? Would persistence change God's sovereign mind? Based on these relational stories and the amount of space devoted to discussion on relationship, the key is not merely persistence, but more importantly relationship. Luke 11:11–13 gives very clear answer by a parable about the relationship between fathers and children. The parable came from a common human condition (Luke 11:11, 13).

The parable is quite humorous if we think about the images. The fish looks like a snake and the egg looks like a scorpion. Jesus' vivid humor gets to the heart of the matter: only fish and eggs are good for the children. God the Father knows best simply because he is analogically similar to the ancient patriarch who ruled the household with omnipotence. The key issue in the description of fish and egg is whether the request would be good for the children. The benefit does not stop at the individual level because the fatherhood of God in the Lord's Prayer created a new family and a new community. Jesus had always been concerned about community benefit. Community benefit and not self-interest is the foundation, based on Jesus' usage of the word "us" in the Lord's Prayer.

Jesus' concluding remark compares evil human beings to a good God in Luke 11:13, once again moving his argument from the smaller (i.e., human fathers) to the greater (i.e., God the Father). Jesus said that human fathers were "evil" in Luke 11:13. It is easy to blame Jesus for being overly pessimistic about human nature. Within Luke's narratives, neither Luke nor Jesus was saying that every single individual was as evil as possible, but that humanity as a whole (the plural "you") is capable of "evil" when we view some of the bad deeds. When we look at the Roman society, there were many possible manifestations of what Jews would call evil. We can also look at the idea of evil in terms of the Roman system of patronage. The power of the earthly father included selling and exposing unwanted children in Jesus' day. Realistically, Jesus compared various kinds of evil or potential for great evil with the picture of the benevolent father. The begrudging friend in Luke 11:7 existed within the evil system created by evil human beings, but God was much better than anyone within that evil human system. In light of Jesus' society, the metaphor of "father" to describe God conveys perfect goodness.

The concluding saying in Luke 11:13 also has a prophetic meaning that is different from merely God's gift to his physically needy people. Jesus mentioned the Holy Spirit. Obviously, the Spirit had not yet manifested all that took place later on Pentecost. The Spirit's work thus far had been limited more to special people like Jesus and John the Baptist, in Luke's writing. Sure, families of both men also experienced the work of the Spirit, but the idea of receiving the Spirit as a gift still remained foreign. Sometimes in Luke, there's a sense of mystery and foreshadowing regarding the future manifestation of God's great work (in this case, the reception of the Spirit), but at this point in the narrative, no one knew that was coming.

So, within context, Jesus taught first that relationship is more important than requests for physical needs. Second, Jesus taught that prayer could bring a future good that surpasses the present need.

PUTTING THE TEXT IN HISTORY: MEANINGS FOR THE WORLD OF AUTHOR-READERS

When putting this story within the world of Theophilus and Luke, we can safely assume that they knew the system of patronage inside and out. They would know that the friend's unreasonable request deserved a big rejection. They also would know that it took extraordinary guts to ask for something with this kind of timing. They would also wonder if the friend's friend would reap benefit for the owner of the bread, but from the look of it, there would be no benefit, not even interest for the loaf of bread.

This parable showed to Theophilus that relationship with God would far surpass his relationships with his fellow human beings, even if those relationships were based on sacrifice. The parable would be subversive for Theophilus simply because it indirectly commented on the social system under which both Jesus and Theophilus lived. In the kingdom of God, even the best scenarios of the imperial system wouldn't compare well with the way God's kingdom worked.

It is interesting that the comparison of the believer's relationship with God came from human relationships. Even throughout the second comparison between "evil" humans and God, the appeal was to the good deeds of humans. When Jesus drew this comparison, he made the way God treated his children the highest standard of relationships. Theophilus, then, would learn this standard so that it would become part of his own treatment of others. Relationships weren't supposed to derive the most benefit for the self like those of the patron-client relationships, but to benefit others.

The parable was also subversive for Theophilus in a different way. When talking about prayer in terms of relationship, Jesus' teaching points to the difference between Gentile religions and Theophilus's faith. With Gentile religions, many of the believers relied on magical incantation or liturgical formulae to pray to their gods. The idea of a relational faith was missing. Theophilus followed the path of a Jewish faith originating from

47

Judaism that emphasized not so much the formulae or even getting one's needs met, but relationship.

When we compare Matthew's version of the Lord's Prayer and this one, we have a very good reason to believe that the prayer had become a part of the early church liturgy. The early believers could easily have become too used to saying it formulaically, but this teaching about relationship ensured that they would say it in a way to express that relationship with God.

MODERN IMPLICATIONS

The story about relationship most certainly implicates the modern church. We often hear this question in our churches. If God knows everything we need already, why should we ask? The question sounds very logical, but that view of prayer comes from the mentality of utilitarian consumerism. Prayer isn't the means to "get stuff from God." Getting stuff isn't relationship building. That's getting relationship backward. Instead, this parable teaches that God gives because we have a relationship with him. Prayer is relationship building. Imagine a marriage. If married people only go to their spouses in order to get stuff, their relationships will feel more like selfish transactions than real love.

In an age of instant gratification, prayer goes against every instinct modern believers have. Jesus' teaching about the giving of the Spirit as a future event points clearly to the fact that prayer doesn't feed the person who wants instant gratification. Even if something is good, it may not happen immediately. People with different temperaments pray differently, but this teaching points to the human weakness of impatience. Prayer rectifies impatience by building one's faith toward a hopeful future.

The present discussion also implicates the kind of God Christians serve. Many in our day and age want to see God as friend. There's nothing wrong with a "friendship" with God. Yet, Jesus' parable makes the distinction between a friend and God. God is so much better than a friend. Jesus made that point very clear. The metaphor of a father surpasses mere friendship. This fatherly metaphor isn't as popular these days, partly because we live in an egalitarian society and partly because many come from broken families. Even though the earthly father can be abusive and imperfect, the fatherhood Jesus described is the ideal. This father cares perfectly and knows completely what is good for the children. He will answer prayer according to that care and knowledge. So, before we focus too much on

God the Father, God the Friend?

God as friend and not enough on God as father, we need to see what the metaphor does. The metaphor puts the believer under the charge and care of the father who has the best interest of his children in mind. Friendship is so much less without fatherhood.

Besides love toward God, prayer also implicates our love toward fellow humans. The Lord's Prayer puts the fatherhood of God over all those who follow Jesus. The benefit God gave for each individual would affect the entire community. No prayer is complete without understanding and appreciating community concerns. The fact that "our daily bread" becomes part of the parable says something about how we should treat the resources God has given us. If people believe in a generous and benevolent God, their generosity toward one another should reflect that belief.

Preachers must avoid certain pitfalls when preaching out of this passage. The preface of the Lord's Prayer followed by the parable points strongly to God's care and compassion toward his children. Some may want to compare it with Matthew's record of the Lord's Prayer in Matthew 6. Matthew had a different emphasis of looking at prayer as one of the pious deeds of a good Jew (Matthew 6:1). The present record by Luke wasn't dealing with a pious deed, per se. Luke focused much more on God's character. There's no need to harmonize the two accounts.

When preaching out of this passage, pastors should avoid direct comparison between the friend and God. The argument of Jesus was progressing from the lesser picture of the ideal friend to the greater picture of the perfect father. Furthermore, it is important for ministers to be sensitive to their congregation when talking about fatherhood. Many have experienced extreme brokenness in their family lives. Some have even been sexually molested. These are the elephants in the room no one wants to touch. This is the place where they can feel doubly traumatized if the fatherhood of God is not handled well. It's best to first dismiss those badly behaving fathers from the metaphor before exploring the fatherhood of God. Many these days, especially those who are associated with certain conservative wings of Protestantism, are obsessed with the gender debate. In fact, some may even see this engendering of God as being part of the gospel core. These are misguided theological efforts that will only make the gospel seem even more irrelevant. Instead of focusing on the gender of God, we may want to focus on the idea within the metaphor of perfect care and perfect knowledge.

When preaching the sermon, the preacher can use irony by talking about the ideal friend and focusing on it because that is sometimes how people understand God. Then, the preacher is responsible to present a clear picture of how God is not like a friend. At the end, the goal is always for the listeners to deepen their prayer lives in terms of their relationship with God rather than their instant gratification. When talking about prayer, though, we should never neglect to talk about how prayer should change our relationships with each other. That's one aspect Jesus didn't forget. Prayer, then, was never just about relationship with God, but it should also improve human relationships with one another.

REFLECTION QUESTIONS

1. What was so annoying about the friend knocking on the door at midnight in Jesus' society?
2. How does the friendship parable relate to the Lord's Prayer?
3. How does the fatherhood of God differ from friendship?
4. What's the point of prayer if God already knows what we want before we ask?
5. How should our understanding of God's character in prayer change our human relationships?

5

Ambiguous Justice?

TELLING IT DIFFERENT: LUKE 12:13-21

> The land of a certain rich man produced an abundant crop, so he thought to himself, "What should I do, for I have nowhere to store my crops?" Then he said, "I will do this: I will tear down my barns and build bigger ones, and there I will store all my grain and my goods. And I will say to myself, 'You have plenty of goods stored up for many years; relax, eat, drink, celebrate!'" The rich man lived happily ever after.

IN JESUS' AGRARIAN SOCIETY, big harvests were always good news. Grain was the very lifeblood of society and for local landowners. The proper care and storage of grain could potentially reap great wealth for the landowner. On the contrary, if the land had no harvest, many could starve. Even worse, if the landowner squandered any extra crop by not properly taking care of it so that it rotted, then not only would profit be lost, but people would also starve. From the Roman era, there are some records of grain riots when people were facing famine. In this way, landowners not only had responsibility toward their own finances but also toward their society. The story above is quite common based on what was going on in Jesus' time. If everything had been taken care of properly, the rich man would surely have lived happily ever after. A wise landowner would have done nothing different.

Another important bit of data to have when reading this parable is the Greco-Roman ideal of leisure. The gentry class of the Romans prided themselves on leisure in that they had so much stored up that they no longer needed to work. The goal, then, would be to get to the point when one could live comfortably like the gentry class. In modern terms, this man in the parable was financially independent to the degree that he could spend the rest of his life on luxurious vacations with no worries whatsoever. The above narrative would have been a dream for any landowner. The man had finally arrived at the point for which he worked so hard all of his life. With all that in mind, Jesus told a different story, but what exactly was Jesus saying here by telling his story the way he did?

TELLING IT NORMAL: KEY ELEMENTS IN THE STORY

> 13 Then someone from the crowd said to him, "Teacher, tell my brother to divide the inheritance with me." 14 But Jesus said to him, "Man, who made me a judge or arbitrator between you two?" 15 Then he said to them, "Watch out and guard yourself from all types of greed, because one's life does not consist in the abundance of his possessions." 16 He then told them a parable: "The land of a certain rich man produced an abundant crop, 17 so he thought to himself, 'What should I do, for I have nowhere to store my crops?' 18 Then he said, 'I will do this: I will tear down my barns and build bigger ones, and there I will store all my grain and my goods. 19 And I will say to myself, "You have plenty of goods stored up for many years; relax, eat, drink, celebrate!"' 20 But God said to him, 'You fool! This very night your life will be demanded back from you, but who will get what you have prepared for yourself?' 21 So it is with the one who stores up riches for himself, but is not rich toward God."

We typically call this "The Parable of the Rich Fool." The parable starts with the topic of abundance in Luke 12:16–17. This story is very true to the land situation of Jesus' day. Not many owned land. Those who did were immensely rich. This particular rich man had too much. So he built more to store his abundance. In order to store all that, the rich man had to tear down his existing warehouse. After years of earning, he had finally hit a big enough payday to retire. He could now enjoy life for many years by eating, drinking, and being merry (Luke 12:19).

In Jesus' day, people's worldview pointed to God when they experienced agricultural abundance. Even before Jesus came, there were plenty of sacrifices stipulated in the Torah for abundance. Such stipulations would include helping the poor (e.g., Deut 14:28–28; 26:12) and sacrificing to God (e.g., Lev 2). Relationships with the poor and with God were the first priorities regarding harvest. Yet, there's no mention of God in the man's thought. Instead, the man built bigger storage presumably to hoard, and congratulated himself for his accomplishment in Luke 12:18–19. The problem ultimately wasn't abundance. The problem was his mentality, as we can tell from what God said in Luke 12:20. God told him that this very night his life would be demanded of him. He was also called a "fool" indicating his lack of wisdom. Jesus' conclusion is very simple. Those who stored up things for themselves but were not rich toward God were just like this fool. The greatest tragedy was that the man had spent his whole life to come to this moment and he couldn't even enjoy it. The urgency of his death is especially clear because God didn't even let him fulfill his intention to build and banquet. He took the man immediately. In illustrating life and death in this parable, Jesus was not against material riches, but was against poverty in things of the kingdom. The typical attitude of a person who was poor toward God was when someone focused on the things of this life, like the rich fool who thought that he had everything figured out in his life, including when he would die. He ended up with much that only others got to enjoy.

CONTEXT

What does the context tell us about the parable? Just as Jesus had finished giving his disciples advice on dealing with religious authorities, the strangest unrelated response came from a person who wanted to tell his brother to divide his inheritance with him. We shall discuss a bit more about Jesus' advice to his disciples about the future a bit later and see if it is related to the present parable. For now, a man wanted Jesus to arbitrate for him against his brother who apparently hoarded all the wealth. Most likely, the brother was an older brother who inherited all the wealth and was responsible to divide up the wealth fairly and evenly. He wanted Jesus involved in the transaction in Luke 12:13. While Jesus was concerned with the kingdom matter, this man was concerned with practical financial matters. From Luke 12:13, it seems that his brother was with him. All this put Jesus in a tough spot because the narrative gives no indication that Jesus knew what exactly was going on between the two brothers.

How, in fact, did this parable answer the quarrel between the brothers? It answered them magnificently. It removed the focal point from the parties in dispute to God's sovereignty and ethics. The hoarding brother could be like the rich man whose life was cut short only to have others enjoy his abundance. Jesus' message was simple. He wanted the two men to think about God's view of material things and then respond to that view. Jesus didn't want to be the arbiter, not because the issue was unimportant to the victim, but because God's view was already quite clear in terms of greed (Deut 29:19), and would now be made clearer by the parable. To be sure, Jesus had a view, but he wanted them to think with him instead of just coming out on the side of the victim.

In order to appreciate the problem of greed, we must understand further the land ownership situation in Jesus' day. When a landowner failed to share the harvest's leftovers with the poor or distribute possessions fairly, he was in essence trying to make the local economy more and more dependent on him. Given the situation that the first century had many poor tenant farmers and no middle class, his action perfectly fit what Jesus said about greed in Luke 12:15. By his greed, he would essentially enslave his kinsmen. Thus, the parable was a condemnation of the hoarder. In other words, Luke 12:15 points to the greed of the hoarding party within the parable. If one thinks that the gift is the end all and be all, then he will only think of the gift without thinking that there's a Giver (i.e., God). How one handles wealth shows where one's focus is. If the brothers were to focus properly, the dispute would slowly disappear. Jesus' message can be summed up in this simple way, "You can't take it with you. Don't hoard. Share!" A kingdom view of possessions is surely needed to solve similar disputes and issues. The parable introduces the fact that one has no control over tomorrow, let alone years from now. That inability to control the future should inform the way one handles material goods.

Luke 12:21 is the grand summary for the parable, as Jesus generalized his teaching for "whoever stores up riches for himself." The parable was no longer applicable just to the brothers but was now applicable to the listening disciples as well. We should also summarize what Jesus meant when he said that the rich man was storing up things for himself. First, Jesus was not against savings, per se. Second, Jesus was talking about the goal of economic dominance being the enjoyment of luxury. The poverty of the rich man was his ethical ruthlessness due to his shortsighted view toward God. In the parable, to be poor toward God meant to be cruel toward fellow humans. In reverse, to be rich toward God meant to be just to other human beings, knowing that ultimately God controls time, talent, and treasure. God would be the judge between the arguing parties.

Ambiguous Justice?

At this point, we ought to bring the previous context of Luke 12:4–12 into the discussion to appreciate Luke's composition of the entire event. These weren't just the same events, but these were also related topics. We must move from the rich man's fate of death to the earlier discourse about the disciples' future in Luke 12:4–12. Those who hoarded wealth would not be ready for persecution that would come against kingdom citizens. Not being ready made them non-citizens. Jesus warned his disciples because they needed to be ready to lose everything. The hoarding rich fool would not be able to face such a challenge. The entire narrative completely makes sense in every part. This emphasis on shortness of life also matches the overall Lukan travel narrative as an illustration of how short life could indeed be. Jesus was traveling to Jerusalem to meet his fate for his own short life. Jesus lived his life with the distinct possibility that it might be cut short, so that his disciples would follow his lead. In such a short span, Jesus had more urgent matters than hoarding wealth.

More contextual reading will help us gain a fuller picture of Jesus' teaching being framed by Luke. The next section Luke 12:22–53 flows naturally from the previous teachings about the rich fool. As the rich fool started the discussion about an eternal view of material possessions, Jesus now continued with his disciples on the same topic. The passage started with "then" in Luke 12:22, possibly pointing back to the rich fool parable. In fact, we can translate the beginning of Luke 12:22 as "but" showing a contrasting life against the other life that was poor toward God.

Jesus continued by speaking about worry in Luke 12:22–23. Jesus' discussion with the disciples starts with "therefore" which means that the previous answer to the man in the crowd has sparked this relevant discussion. While anxiety is part of human nature, it is not healthy as part of one's lifestyle. While worrying is not a sin, it does betray possible misplacement of priorities, as Jesus would go on to show.

In Luke 12:22–23, Jesus mentioned some of the things people worried about: food and clothing. What troubled the rich man previously now troubled everyone including Jesus' not-so-rich disciples. While the rich man in the previous parable had a problem of abundance, the average person might have a problem of shortage. The problem of material is universal. Jesus was not here talking about the concerns of having excesses like the rich fool, but the simple problem of every peasant, putting food on the table and putting clothes on the body. Jesus was not saying that these were unimportant, but that life was about much more than these basic issues.

55

Jesus then used an illustration from the animal kingdom in Luke 12:24. The very same kind of teaching also occurs in Matthew 6:25–34, in a slightly different form. In Luke, Jesus used the raven, a bird that was considered unclean because of its dietary habits (Lev 11:15). Such a worthless bird shouldn't receive any attention from God, but it did. Jesus said that the bird didn't need to do the farming and storage. In fact, Jesus highlighted the bird's worthlessness in Luke 12:24b compared to the disciples' supreme worth as children under God's care (cf. Luke 12:30, 32). There is no need to worry. With the raven, Jesus talked about food, and now with the lilies, Jesus talked about clothing in Luke 12:27–28. With the lilies, the logic is the same as the raven analogy. The lilies didn't have to try hard to look great, even greater than the clothing on Solomon's body in Luke 12:27.

The brilliance of the analogies comes from their absurdity. The disparity between the raven and the farmer who needed to store was already great. The disparity between the lilies and Solomon was even greater. The raven was an unclean bird but at least it was from the animal world. While the farmer systematically built storehouses and stored food, the raven could at least hunt for rotten corpses. While Solomon could change his own clothes and had others weave for him, the lilies were plants. Plants could do nothing. Yet, the disciples were more valuable than both the ravens and the lilies. The analogies were not downgrading the importance of the well-planned farmer or the wise Solomon, but they were meant to show that both the farmer and Solomon had limits when God's care came into the picture. The greatest absurdity is obviously the final analogy of grass in Luke 12:28, in comparison to the disciples. The grass was to be burnt like rubbish. The disciples were not. Grass is the most worthless item in the analogies, compared with ravens and lilies. God even cared about the most worthless. How much more would God care for the disciples? God's care was supremely expressed in nature.

By using such analogies, Jesus called for the release of such preoccupation by noting first that pagans run after the same things, and by calling disciples to give away their possessions in the subsequent verses. The importance of the analogies comes from God's role. Jesus said that the hoarding of wealth was something that "the pagans" did (Luke 12:30). The word for pagan literally means "Gentiles." The Gentiles were the ones who did not have Israel's value from YHWH. Jesus was basically contrasting the Gentile value system against the kingdom value system, showing how one excludes the other. In the context of what Jesus said, these were people who did not belong to Israel the way the disciples did. Thus, the disciples would be deemed absolutely abnormal for acting like Gentiles in hoarding their wealth. The continuous thoughts about material possessions show both a foolish (cf. Luke 12:20) and pagan value, but continuous seeking of the kingdom values would show a faith in God's care (Luke 12:31). What kingdom values was Jesus talking about? Luke 12:33 provides the answer. While the location for the treasure was in "heaven" (wherever that might be), the investment on earth would be the poor. Luke 12:34 says that wherever one's heart is, there also lies his treasures. The heart then belonged to both heaven and the poor. The way to express heaven was to benefit the poor down here.

Within the context of what Jesus had said, we can summarize what Luke tried to teach through the recording of this parable. Luke first showed that all possessions were temporary, especially in light of the future persecution. Second, the handling of possessions demonstrates one's faith and priorities. Third, and this is in complete agreement with the Old Testament teachings on helping the poor, the best way to express that faith in the kingdom was to use possessions to benefit those who are in need. The problem of the rich fool has much to do with all these three lessons. His possessions would weigh him down so much that he wouldn't be able to give them up for the kingdom if persecution came. The absence of God in his thinking also shows that his priorities weren't in line with God's. Signaling to us his religious poverty, he never even thought about the poor.

PUTTING THE TEXT IN HISTORY: MEANINGS FOR THE WORLD OF AUTHOR-READERS

This parable is precisely relevant to Theophilus. In hearing the story, he would identify with the complexity of inheritance and wealth. In his society, the problem of wealth plagued both the rich and the poor. The rich had so much that they had to do what the rich man did. The poor had so little that they had to worry about what they didn't have. The struggle was real. Jesus told this story within that culture.

As a man of many resources, Theophilus had many who depended on him. As a man with power, he could practice or neglect justice. His place in society was important. While his society depended on reciprocation of favors and his power depended on his favors, this block of material taught him that he needed to dispense favor freely. The entire parable and the surrounding material were subversive to his world.

As a man of faith, Theophilus received the challenge to live his life with God in its center. Yet, this was not some ivory tower ideal or theology. This block of material was grounded in the way Theophilus lived everyday. The way he lived expressed the God he believed. Instead of amassing wealth like the typical rich man, he ought to give it away to the poor. This required a determination to lower himself in the social hierarchy. If his assets dipped below a certain minimal amount, the future of his children would be at risk. The damage his faith might do to his social status could become irreparable, but Jesus gave the assurance that he had treasures stored in heaven for him.

MODERN IMPLICATIONS

The parable of the rich fool is interesting because we often think in terms of spirituality about how a person handles his material goods, but this is about much more. The parable is also about control. The obsession to control all that one has in order to keep getting richer is folly. In this case, the way the man handles his abundance shows his spiritual condition. Jesus' condemnation was not about dishonest gain. There's no such hint here. His negative assessment deals with the fact that the man has not once been rich toward God. God wasn't mentioned in his monologue with himself. He was a godless man. When we think we can control our future, we no longer think about God. In reality, the parable and the surrounding material also teach that God controls the future.

In Jesus' day, there were no atheists, but people could live as if they were atheists. People like this rich man had the ability to let possessions squeeze God out of their lives. With abundance, the excessive material could be handled by either a savings plan (like a bigger barn) or by giving it away. Making a bigger container to store the excess seems to contradict kingdom values in that it does not take into consideration what God wants. Based on Old Testament stipulations, the leftovers in the field were to be given to the poor (Deut 29:19). Is this the folly Jesus talked about?

Today, we have a similar problem. Every year, lots of food is wasted in either grocery stores or restaurants in the developed world. The parable certainly speaks loudly to all rich Christians who contribute to unwise usage of resources. What would God's view be? That is a necessary question to ask. The story is about God's sovereignty. Ultimately, control of possessions is not humans' but God's. The wise will acknowledge that sovereignty. Material abundance obligates a person to be more and not less mindful of God and God's value system. Otherwise, we repeat the story of the rich fool.

One very important aspect that a lot of commentators haven't noticed is the discussion about hardship that precedes the parable. The teaching talks about the hardship disciples will someday face, even losing their lives. How in fact is hardship related to material goods? When faced with the choice to give up everything for the faith or to hoard everything and compromise the faith, the disciples will quickly discover the bottom line of their priorities. When I view a lot of Western churches and their missions, this parable surprisingly applies perfectly. Many Western megachurches have invested in missions work within countries that clearly violate human rights. For the sake of their mission and not losing their resources, they don't only fail to say anything about such systemic evil; they inevitably cooperate with evil governments. The very same can be said in Hong Kong where I worked for some time. So many big organizations, churches, and even seminaries, don't want to make statements against the oppressive regime of China. Why? It is because too much financial and missional interest is at stake. All such compromises are essentially atheistic because they don't have God's interest in mind.

Here are some suggestions for preachers. The block of material surrounding the parable is too much to preach in a thirty- to forty-minute sermon on Sunday morning. Therefore the preacher must pick and choose the kind of presentation that will work within that time frame. Timeliness these days is next to godliness in church. The story of the rich fool is fairly straightforward. The problem is clear and the conclusion is even clearer with God's condemnation. What is unclear is how the surrounding material contributes. For example, the absence of God in the whole thinking process and the serious presence of God in the surrounding material deserves to be mentioned. Instead of focusing only on the negative for this rich man, illustrations can come from surrounding material about God's care and faith. We don't have to use ancient illustrations like Jesus did. We can also use modern illustrations that demonstrate a loving father who cares for his children. The negative aspect also needs mentioning. The material before the rich fool parable clearly talks about hardship that comes because of faith. The neglect of this hardship can easily cause one to focus only on one's own prosperity. The background of the Old Testament regarding the poor also can help illustrate how the rich man was indeed a fool, as the following passage talks about helping the poor as a means of investing in the kingdom. We have to be very careful however when telling this parable because it can give the wrong impression that Jesus was not in favor of any planning for the future or a having a savings plan. Those weren't the concern of this parable. If the preacher explains the above elements, the audience won't think that Jesus was somehow teaching against a sound financial plan.

REFLECTION QUESTIONS

1. Was Jesus against saving up for the future?
2. What was the problem of the rich fool?
3. How does the background of the rich fool shows that he's made a mistake?
4. How does the passage preceding it relate to the rich fool?
5. How does the passage following the story relate to the rich fool?
6. Why is the comparison of the disciples to ravens, lilies, and even grass of the field powerful?

6

Faithful Service and Unfaithful Servants

TELLING IT DIFFERENT: LUKE 12:35–48

> Blessed are those slaves whom their master finds alert when he returns! I tell you the truth, he will dress himself to serve, have them take their place at the table, and will come and wait on them! Even if he comes in the second or third watch of the night and finds them alert, blessed are those slaves! But understand this: If the owner of the house had known at what hour the thief was coming, he would not have let his house be broken into. Who then is the faithful and wise manager, whom the master puts in charge of his household servants, to give them their allowance of food at the proper time? Blessed is that slave whom his master finds at work when he returns. I tell you the truth, the master will put him in charge of all his possessions.

THIS IS A HAPPY story. Ancient slaves worked at the bidding of their masters. In fact, when we look closely at some parts of Roman law, slaves weren't even considered humans but were property of their master. Now, Jesus was talking to a Jewish audience. Among Jews, ideally, no Jew should enslave another Jew because they were all children from the same Abrahamic family. Thus, most likely, Jesus was speaking about the Roman law that most of his audience would have understood. After all, the Roman Empire was a slave society (i.e., a society built on slave labor).

The above story fits perfectly the way slaves were to behave. Their job was to be ready to serve the master. The only way for a slave to advance was to be in charge of more of his master's possessions. A very wealthy master in those days was so full of possessions that he could hardly manage everything. He relied on his faithful slaves to manage the estate, even to manage his other slaves. Data from Roman literature tells us that the lowliest slaves were the rural farm slaves who were farthest away from the master, who used ruthless stewards to manage them. The more powerful slaves would stay closer to the master's home, most likely near the city where he conducted his business. More responsibility also meant closer access to the powerful master. More access to power would result in more personal advantage. The faithful slave, most of all, was the wise servant who knew what was good for him and followed through with good behavior. Jesus told the story differently though. What exactly was Jesus saying here by telling his story the way he did?

TELLING IT NORMAL: KEY ELEMENTS IN THE STORY

> 37 "It will be good for those servants whose master finds them watching when he comes. Truly I tell you, he will dress himself to serve, will have them recline at the table and will come and wait on them. 38 It will be good for those servants whose master finds them ready, even if he comes in the middle of the night or toward daybreak. 39 But understand this: If the owner of the house had known at what hour the thief was coming, he would not have let his house be broken into. 40 You also must be ready, because the Son of Man will come at an hour when you do not expect him."
>
> 41 Peter asked, "Lord, are you telling this parable to us, or to everyone?"
>
> 42 The Lord answered, "Who then is the faithful and wise manager, whom the master puts in charge of his servants to give them their food allowance at the proper time? 43 It will be good for that servant whom the master finds doing so when he returns. 44 Truly I tell you, he will put him in charge of all his possessions. 45 But suppose the servant says to himself, 'My master is taking a long time in coming,' and he then begins to beat the other servants, both men and women, and to eat and drink and get drunk. 46 The master of that servant will come on a day when he does not expect him and at an hour he is not aware of. He will cut him to pieces and assign him a place with the unbelievers.
>
> 47 "The servant who knows the master's will and does not get ready or does not do what the master wants will be beaten with many blows. 48 But the one who does not know and does things deserving punishment will be beaten with few blows. From

Faithful Service and Unfaithful Servants

everyone who has been given much, much will be demanded; and from the one who has been entrusted with much, much more will be asked."

The plot of the parable is simple. Jesus started with the command to be dressed and ready. The command in Luke 12:35 shows that the entire episode addresses the disciples collectively without exceptions, just like what Jesus started in Luke 12:22. Readiness includes girding one's loins. The idea of girding the loins is to shorten one's clothing to free the legs for action. When one was banqueting, there was no need to shorten the toga. The long flowing toga however inhibited movement of the legs. That's why when we look at ancient carvings, the slaves' clothing was always somewhat shorter than their master's. A worker needed to shorten the lower part of the clothing by cinching up the belt. The purpose of such readiness was for service of the master. The servants knew that the master would be coming back. So, they dressed and waited for his return from a wedding. The story had to do with the absence and the unannounced return of the master much like the return of the Son of Man.

Why were lamps ready? They were ready just in case the master unexpectedly came back at night. Jesus assumed that the master, after attending someone's wedding banquet, came from a long way because the servants would have to be ready to feed the hungry master. Even if he came at a strange hour in the morning (Luke 12:38) when everyone would be sleeping, the master expected service.

The additional explanation in this parable comes in Luke 12:39–40, where Jesus used a thief to illustrate the unexpected. This explanation likens the coming of the Son of Man to a thief who could break into a house. The owner of such a house would be ready for the thief. The servants didn't know when the master would come, but they knew he would come. The owner of the house didn't know whether a thief would come, but he was anxious not to lose his possessions. In the same way, the slave who managed the master's possessions ought to have the same faithful alertness. The disciples must take the same attitude.

Peter now interrupted Jesus to ask whether Jesus was telling this parable to the disciples or to everyone around in Luke 12:41. Apparently, many were listening. Jesus continued with the slave parable in Luke 12:42–48.

This parable continues to discuss the relationship between the slave to the absent master in regard to stewardship. The faithful servant in Luke 12:42 apparently was the head steward over other slaves, to distribute food. If this servant were faithful in doing so, he would be put in charge of greater things (Luke 12:44). Jesus' parable coheres well with what he talked about before in his discussion about material goods in Luke 12:16–21. To be faithful with the goods means to be like a faithful steward, distributing them wisely and not becoming occupied by them (cf. Luke 12:33). In our society, having more responsibility might not sound like much fun, but in Jesus' society of honor and shame, the more responsibility one had, the greater respect one received and greater power one gained.

While the section of Luke 12:42–44 depicts faithful stewardship, the section of Luke 12:45–48 depicts unfaithful stewardship. Luke 12:45 starts with "if," a unique form of the word in Greek, to denote only a hypothetical situation of a head slave abusing slaves under him. By stating his case using this hypothetical "if," Jesus was basically saying that in order for a steward to be this unfaithful, that steward must have been completely foolish. The degree of unfaithfulness was a near impossibility in Jesus' world. In a similar manner, a true disciple wouldn't be this lax.

It is easy to condemn the master's cruel treatment of the slave using our modern perspectives, but Jesus was just showing the grave possibility of severe punishment in the ancient world. The steward who was murdered in Luke 12:46 was clearly a slave. Masters held the rights over their slaves' lives because slaves were property in the Roman system. An unfaithful slave would be assigned to a place of harsh punishment where all the other unfaithful slaves went, namely the graveyard. That place spells death for the slave. There is no assumption that the unfaithful needed to be alive. They were just assigned a place, most likely a place of destruction, much like the rubbish heap for dead bodies and rubbish outside of Jerusalem.

In ending the parable with such a harsh conclusion, Jesus blended the parable into a pregnant theological statement. By keeping in mind this cruel possibility of utter destruction, no steward in his right mind would become this horrendously unfaithful. Did Jesus answer the question Peter posed? Jesus included everyone in Luke 12:48b. In other words, while Jesus spoke directly to the disciples here, his words were for anyone who could hear him within earshot. The more they heard, the more responsible they would have to be. This rhetorical move also addresses Peter's question in a different way because Peter seems quite pleased to be told such teachings. In effect, Jesus warned Peter especially not to become so pleased but be vigilant in obedience. The more Peter knew, the greater accountability required. The degree of punishment is proportional to knowledge.

Faithful Service and Unfaithful Servants

CONTEXT

Let's review the context in which Jesus told the parable. We have already discussed the context from the last chapter, but it's worth a brief review. The central issue in the surrounding context is control, especially in light of the coming of the Son of Man. Ultimately, since Jesus told the people what would happen, God was the only one in control. How then were the disciples to respond to this? They were to use their possessions wisely to benefit those in need, knowing that they would be judged according to what God had given to them. The moral is actually very simple. Now that same paradigm ought to be applied to the present parable because Luke 12:35 doesn't indicate a break in Jesus' speech at all. Instead, the present parable concludes what was said above it "For where your treasure is, there your heart will be also."

PUTTING THE TEXT IN HISTORY: MEANINGS FOR THE WORLD OF AUTHOR-READERS

Theophilus could relate to all tales about masters and household slaves. He was a master. He probably couldn't conceive of the fact that some of the slaves might be unfaithful when he went away from his home for business. Their unfaithfulness would cause him to lose face. Their behavior would earn them an extreme reprimand. In a shame and honor society, once a master lost the respect of his slaves, all sorts of irregularities could happen in the household. Theophilus knew that Jesus was describing a dangerous and shameful scenario. Bad discipleship with horrible management of God-given resources is a dangerous and shameful scenario. Theophilus could well understand the feeling the Son of Man had when he would come back. After all, "the Son of Man will come at an hour when you do not expect him" (Luke 12:40). Theophilus would do well to heed the warning to use his resources wisely, knowing that resource distribution would be the standard by which he would be judged.

When faced with such a challenge, Theophilus's world had to be radically subverted. He was someone with status and a future in his society. Yet, due to the new life he had discovered by following Jesus and his teachings, he no longer had full rights to his own resources. Being under Jesus made him a slave. Theophilus then would have to depend on Jesus. He would have to serve Jesus the way his household slaves served a master. He would reciprocate toward Jesus by giving generously to others. This also subverted his exclusive loyalty to the empire. The Roman sense of history was dependent on the Roman peace maintained by its power, its rulers, and its military. He no longer could adhere to the value that Caesar was the supreme lord. He now had to acknowledge that the Son of Man had become his Lord. No matter what dynastic change was happening, the Son of Man remained the Lord over Theophilus. Jesus' sense of history points toward a greater purpose in history, in which Jesus was the main player in God's great plan.

MODERN IMPLICATIONS

The modern reader can hardly imagine slavery as a part of a parable. Modern Western readers are used to an egalitarian society where people perceive themselves to be autonomous individuals. Yet, each person has a degree of obligation to someone else. For instance, if we go to work, we feel obligated to our bosses. Even if we're bosses, we have a social obligation to our employees and our society. If we break such social conventions, there'll be consequences. The consequences of not following the rules of our society can result in all sorts of losses. With work, it can result in financial loss. If the job market is good, the boss who manages badly will lose human resources through high turnover. As a result, the cost of training new employees will start to cut into the profit margin that the company may need during lean years. Obligation then is part of the human condition. Let's say I'm financially independent and drive around in a super car—like a Ferrari. I may think that I'm free from obligations, but if I choose to act like I'm in an F-1 Grand Prix race and if I'm not alert to the presence of a police car, I may end up in prison. Obligations.

With obligations of course comes alertness. Alertness requires us to understand to whom we're obligated. For instance, I don't want the police to catch me speeding. I'm aware that I'm obligated to the police. Socially, that police officer is above me, no matter how rich I am. In this parable, the idea of obligation points toward judgment and the future for the disciple. This challenges us to develop a kind of awareness that benefits us in how we invest our lives. When we think about investment, we think about gains. Jesus spoke in such financial terms in an ironic manner to show that obligation toward God calls the disciple to give away resources to those in need.

As Jesus was talking, he was not talking to a lot of rich people. He was talking to his disciples who came from various social economic classes.

Thus, this applies across the board. Would this also apply to the way we do church? This is a complex question that deserves a book-length treatment, but it's a conversation that needs to happen. Quite often, we use our money in church to accomplish things "within" the church, but no so much outside of it. If our church is made up of upwardly mobile members (not all churches are, of course), then we serve our needs based on our own wealth rather than serving someone else in a lower social economic class. Based on this parable, all those who serve the Master, including those in the church, ought to do what the Master had told them to do. In the present case, the alertness or readiness has nothing to do with waiting for the coming of the Son of Man while sitting on our proverbial hands. Jesus was talking about alertness to do one's duty to help those who are in need. The further seriousness of this teaching has much to do with the amount of knowledge people have (Luke 12:48). Those who know better need to get going.

Preachers can preach this parable easily, especially if they interpret the parable based on the context just prior. They might have to correct the stargazing end-time dreamer who reads the present parable as a passive waiting game. Preachers should strongly preach against such an interpretation of the parable because it goes directly against its real meaning. The pitfall of preaching this parable in such a way is that the church will eventually start the conversation about what it means to be obedient to God in resource distribution. This parable is horribly subversive in every aspect because it goes against the usual "business model" of so many successful churches. Jesus was not looking to measure success based purely on statistics. He was rather looking for radical obedience that will end up in sacrificial investment in the kingdom.

REFLECTION QUESTIONS

1. Why would the conventions of slavery speak to Jesus' audience?
2. What were the advantages of being a higher-ranked slave?
3. Why is the parable not only about alertness but also about wisdom?
4. How is a slave parable relevant in our day?
5. What unlikely interpretations can arise from such a parable?
6. How would obedience to this parable impact your life and your church?

7

The Greatness of Smallness

TELLING IT DIFFERENT: LUKE 13:18-21

> What is the kingdom of God like? To what should I compare it? It is like a mustard seed that that wind blows around and it lands randomly in a garden. It grew and became a tree, and the wild birds nested in its branches.

THIS STORY IS VERY much in accordance the way farming worked in Jesus' day. While mustard plant was probably useful, it was also everywhere in the land. To simplify matters, the mustard plant wasn't just easy to plant, but it was also easy to grow. It could grow into a very large bush, even perhaps up to ten feet. At the very least, the seed could grow into a size where birds could enjoy its shade in the hot summer heat.

If told this way, what would the parable mean? It would mean something quite simple: that the kingdom of God grew with some great force from small to large. It naturally grew because of all the forces around it. Certainly, there's an aspect of this growth in Luke's story (e.g., Luke 12:1), but what exactly was Jesus saying here by telling his story the way he did?

TELLING IT NORMAL: KEY ELEMENTS IN THE STORY

> 18 Thus Jesus asked, "What is the kingdom of God like? To what should I compare it? 19 It is like a mustard seed that a man took and sowed in his garden. It grew and became a tree, and the wild birds nested in its branches."

The Greatness of Smallness

> 20 Again he said, "To what should I compare the kingdom of God? 21 It is like yeast that a woman took and mixed with three measures of flour until all the dough had risen."

Before we jump to any conclusions, it is important to note that Matthew 13:31–35 is a parallel to the present passage. I have written on this in *Right Kingdom*.[1] So, I won't rehash the plot in any detail, but let me summarize what Matthew was saying before we dive into the parable and its context here because Luke seems to be saying something else.

The basic plot line is exactly the same as Matthew's recording of it. It is the context that makes it drastically different in Luke. What then is the plotline? Basically, the deliberate planting of a single seed by the sower seems unusual, especially that such an insignificant seed with insignificant size could serve enough function for a sower to plant it in a field. Thus, the kingdom in its seemingly accidental growth was no accident.

I skipped the second parable in my different retelling of the story because it adds to the first parable. Without it, the story seems quite random. The second parable shows how a small amount of yeast made the dough grow. The amount of dough would be about fifty pounds. The telling of this parable is significant in that it shows the typical household scene of a woman working hard. The visible yeast became invisible through her work. She didn't just plant the presumably small yeast into the dough. She worked the yeast into this large amount of dough, presumably to make a very large meal for the family. After all, how would a few family members finish a fifty pounds of bread? She was doing it for the entire family for a few meals. The picture however shows that the kingdom was not only planned but also laborious. Kneading yeast into a fifty-pound dough was no small task. So, the first parable about planning moves nicely into the second parable about hard work.

CONTEXT

It is entirely wrong to read the parable without the context of Luke 13:10–17. The location of Luke 13:10 was the synagogue, where a healing took place. It was a place of religion and social interaction for all Jews. Here's where a woman crippled by a spirit was healed. Luke didn't give her name or rank in society, but we can probably assume that she was not viewed with any high

---

1. Tsang, *Right Kingdom*, 31–38.

rank in that society. Luke spent a lot of time talking about her ailment. A spirit had disabled her for eighteen years. The Greek of Luke 13:11 actually can mean "has a spirit." The spirit could have been a demonic spirit because Jesus said in Luke 13:16 that she was under the bondage of Satan. How she ended up in the synagogue was a mystery. Perhaps, her presence wasn't terribly disruptive. The focal point is the length of her misery, eighteen years. Her ailment caused her to be unable to stand up, according to Luke 13:11.

Jesus' statement to her in Luke 13:12 pronounced her change of physical state by setting her free. The text clearly shows that she didn't request the liberation, but Jesus gave her freedom anyway. His words were followed by the action of his touch in Luke 13:13. The healing was immediate rather than gradual. Immediacy of healing is often linked with the power of Jesus' healing in Luke (Luke 5:25; 8:44; etc.). Her reaction was to stand up and praise God. Her reaction was normal for the sick being healed or those who stood by to see the miracle (cf. Luke 5:25–26; 7:16). Instead of praising God like the average character in Luke's healing stories, the religious leader of that community pronounced a condemnation against Jesus for healing on the Sabbath in Luke 13:14. Their anger was over someone doing something wrong, probably based on a certain interpretation of labor in Exodus 20:8–11 and Deuteronomy 5:12–15.

Based on the narrator's description, could putting a hand on a woman and healing her be considered labor? The description of Jesus' work shows its effortlessness. However, the synagogue leader focused not on the effort but on the result, stating that there were six days where Jesus could heal but not on the Sabbath day. This statement implies that the woman possibly came to the synagogue during the week as well. Since the synagogue was the place for alms giving, she might have been there to beg. Yet, was this leader actually aware of her presence, or was he assuming her presence on other days of the week? The important thing, according to the narrator, was that he was indignant because of the healing on the Sabbath. By addressing Jesus and not the people, he sensed that Jesus wanted to do this healing as a direct confrontation to the way of the synagogue.

Jesus then responded by calling not only the leader, but also others, hypocrites because obviously the religious leaders also convinced many in the crowd that they were right. By comparing the healing of the woman to the untying of animals on the Sabbath in Luke 13:15–16, Jesus drew on one similarity between animals and the woman, in order to emphasize the differences. The similarity between the two would be that both the animals and the women were bound. The differences were that the animals only got tied up temporarily while Satan bound the woman for eighteen years. Furthermore, the animals couldn't be as valuable as the woman who was a daughter of Abraham. We can only argue that animals were more valuable if we consider them purely in financial terms, and Jesus already condemned such a worldview in Luke 12. Jesus argued his case from the lesser (animals) to the greater (humans) with reference to the Abrahamic covenant. If the lesser was permissible, the greater certainly should have been. In Luke 13:17, the narrator says that all of Jesus' opponents were humiliated while the people were delighted. The irony of this story is that the religious leader would prefer Satan to bind this woman one more day than for Sabbath to be violated.

It is easy for modern Christians to see this as an anti-Judaism story, but the discussion wasn't about how bad Judaism was. Instead, it was discussing an interpretation and even a debate within Judaism of how the faithful should follow certain laws. It has nothing to do with Judaism being evil, but has everything to do with how God's will ought to be practiced within God's laws. It is important to note that Jesus' relationship with religious leaders wasn't always negative in Luke. There were times when some other leaders were friendly with Jesus (cf. Luke 7:3–6). Some even cared for Jesus' own safety (cf. Luke 13:31). In this case the violation of a certain interpretation of the Sabbath law had offended a local leader. The conflict was not mainly Jesus versus Judaism. The conflict was Jesus speaking and acting against a certain interpretation within certain corner of Judaism.

When reading this parable, it is also important to see the woman as having dignity. Although the yeast didn't seem significant, it could well become important in expanding the bread and feeding more people. In the same way, this woman's influence was like the yeast. In her seeming insignificance, her healing had demonstrated to everyone, including those within religious leadership, how true religion ought to be lived out.

How did the seed parable apply to the healing miracle? Obviously, Jesus' work was the work of the kingdom of God. His present work was something insignificant like the mustard seed, and certainly his patient, the crippled woman, was very insignificant. The planting of this work was also unusual like a singular seed being deliberately planted by a sower. The healing of this insignificant woman had huge impact like the mustard seed. It was also unconventional like a man planting a singular seed. Yet in its unconventional way, the healing was also deliberate. It brought out the theological debate about Sabbath, but also granted this woman significance in her insignificant social role. It also demonstrated that the Sabbath had a true meaning and wasn't what the religious leader imagined. The original seed of healing then had yielded a relatively large crop. Still larger things were to come. The kingdom work here shows Jesus occupying a contested space and making something of it. The healing is a microscopic glimpse of larger kingdom impact. We must now see how the second parable links well with the story of the Sabbath healing.

How did the yeast parable pertain to the healing of the woman on Sabbath? In fact, the humble woman who was healed in such a significant way shows how the smallness of the kingdom had become so huge. The deed was done for the lowly much like the seed or the yeast, but the impact would be gigantic. Perhaps Jesus was saying that his kingdom work was not going to be easy especially after the healing took place, much like when the yeast was originally put into the flour. Much opposition would continue against Jesus' work for the little people. Whatever followed would be hard work, but its final effect would be much greater than a mere debate over Sabbath and healing. Indeed, this was certainly the case when Jesus lost his life at the end. At the same time, without that death, the kingdom work would not have been accomplished. The parables then were both analogical and prophetic. Both parables had to do with something small affecting the very surface it touched. Both were visibly insignificant at first because we could neither see the seed in the ground nor the yeast in the dough. Yet, the ending point changed the way some people looked at the Sabbath and the significance of a lowly human being. Even greater would be Jesus' work later when he died on the cross.

PUTTING TEXT IN HISTORY: MEANINGS FOR THE WORLD OF AUTHOR-READERS

Theophilus had some connections to the synagogues, as I noted in the introduction. He had a good enough understanding of Sabbath law to warrant Luke's continued discussion about Sabbath law in Luke 14:1–14, a passage we shall address shortly. Theophilus, then, would have to navigate between what he understood to be God's will or God's law versus its application.

In a world of give and take, favors and disfavor, honor and shame, Theophilus understood the importance of human lives in financial terms. People were either useful or useless. The crippled woman was about as useless as they came. She was one of the lowliest people of their society. She had no financial worth. However, Jesus healed her. When Jesus compared her to the animal, clearly the animal had more financial worth. Yet, she had greater worth according to Jesus simply because she was the child of Abraham. Within the Judaism of Jesus' day, human worth was part of the law. That's why the religious leader and his supporters were humiliated in Luke 13:17. They didn't dare to say that the animal was worth more than the woman. Luke's story subverted Theophilus's social values by recognizing great worth in a seemingly worthless character, all because Jesus gave her the worth. Thus, when looking at his own social interactions in light of God's law, Theophilus had gained a compass for setting his life's direction. He ought to stop thinking about human worth in terms of money but start thinking in terms of their inherent worth given by Jesus.

Like many stories with social implications, Theophilus would be severely challenged to associate himself with such seemingly worthless people. If he were to do so, he would also risk the advantages he held by not associating with such people. Yet, the small things, much like the mustard seed or the yeast, built the kingdom. Such small things would reap a long-term harvest, though in the short term, this kind of investment would appear counterproductive. Yet, like both the seed and the yeast, the smallness was deliberate. Theophilus, then, also ought to be deliberate about his association with the small people in anticipation of a great harvest in the future.

MODERN IMPLICATIONS

If there's ever a story that has major implications for the modern church, this pair of parables may be it. The modern manifestation of faith is as much about the business of religion as it is about a real relationship between God and humans. The biggest problem with the business of religion is vested interests. If we look at the way some of the popular bookstores responded to Alex Malarkey's retraction of the veracity of his book, *The Boy Who Came Back from Heaven*, we can see that the business of religion is alive and well. Just in recent times, two or three separate cases of publication scandal in the Christian publishing world (one having to do with massive plagiarism and the other having to do with the boy who supposedly went to heaven) reveal our love for money and fame rather than our love for integrity and relationship.

Right Parables, Wrong Perspectives

Many popular bookstores refused to pull the books off their shelves because they would lose money. Some eventually pulled the books more than half a year after the scandal broke in the plagiarism case. The businesses simply didn't care if the lives of readers would be affected in both cases. Many will continue to protect the guilty because the machine needs to prop up big names to build its profit margin in the name of the kingdom. Some wanted the scandal to go away quietly so that business could carry on as usual. There have been other scandalous cases, and from the example of recent history there'll be others in the future.

Big financial profit is all very American. We want to see success. In fact, we lust after the appearance of success and orderliness, much like those who argued with Jesus in the story, so that our peaceful success won't be disturbed. Sometimes, we even hit the mother lode, such as Malarkey's heavenly tale, based on pure luck—until we run out of luck. Then we try to find the next big thing, much like the parable without the yeast story. We may want to have the kind of success that just blows up like random mustard seeds. Luke's story condemns such an ethos. He was looking toward hard work among the oppressed.

Considering people only in terms of financial gain or loss was hideous for Luke's Jesus. The kingdom was about doing something for the little ones so that they would receive their God-given dignity and worth. That's the point of these parables. It's never about profiteering from the little ones or from big corporate machines. It's always first and foremost about doing the little things that would lead to the proper results. Doing the little things can be hard work much like the woman kneading a huge lump of dough. Those who value finance over lives ultimately want to do little work but get big results. That would be the very opposite of what Jesus wanted in the story.

Speaking on this passage has its own unique challenges. It has its own tradition of people reading Matthew 13 into Luke 13. Although such a tradition is quite popular among many who choose to read a harmonized version of the Gospels, this tradition may not be accurate at all. The tradition basically only celebrates the explosive growth of the kingdom, from being small to being huge. Preachers may have to overcome this triumphalist obstacle at their own risk. Quite often, preachers celebrate their own church growth in reading the text in this popular way, but Jesus was doing the opposite. Truth is worth the risk, though. The narrative clearly links the parables to the healing story before. The best thing perhaps is to read the entire story strategically starting from the healing story. If a preacher has already earned the trust of his or her congregation, then a bit more risky presentation can also put a shock to the system, so to speak. A more subversive way is to look first at the parables themselves before talking about what they really mean in the context of the healing story. At the end, the conclusion should utilize the context of the healing story, making the point that helping the small people was hard work, not because the healing was difficult for Jesus but because certain segment of Judaism was highly resistant to this practice. Overcoming the resistance, then, became the hard work. Traditions die hard, as is evident when such parables are properly preached in traditionalistic congregations. The very risk of preaching this illustrates perfectly these parables.

REFLECTION QUESTIONS

1. Why are Jesus' parables not anti-Judaism?
2. How does the present story different from Matthew 13?
3. How do the parables address the narrative context?
4. How does taking away the yeast story diminish the parable?

8

Kingdom Faux Pas

TELLING IT DIFFERENT: LUKE 14:7-14

> When you are invited to a banquet, go and find the appropriate place for you socially. A man went to a banquet. Upon entering, he found his appropriate seat. The host saw him and welcomed him to his house. They enjoyed the meal together.

IN THE UNITED STATES, the places people sit only matter when the occasion is highly formal. Not so in many parts of the world. In fact, if one were to sit in the wrong seat in northern China, even if that person was a Westerner, he or she would be invited to move to the right place, most likely a much lower place. The seats to the left and right of the host are reserved for the most important guests with the right being the most honored seat. Many Westerners have blundered by sitting in the wrong seat while trying to make a business deal, for example.

The fact of the matter is, most ancient civilizations focused on formality and order because such formality reflected the way their societies functioned. Many such formalities carry over to today. In general, Americans are more casual, but not so the rest of the world. In the story above, the man had found his appropriate place. In order to find his appropriate place, he had to know the host and the guests well enough to understand his place in the hierarchy. Many banquets in Jesus' day involved a lot of people. For people to find their places was not an easy task. Not every table had nameplates the way many modern banquets do today. Nevertheless, there was an implicit hierarchy that everyone was expected to know. This made seating very tricky. To be seated in the wrong place could ruin a relationship. For instance, if one were seated in a higher place than one ought, then people who should have been seated in those seats would become very offended. This could affect both present relationships and future business deals. Social faux pas have consequences. Jesus certainly understood this complexity and told the story differently than above, but what exactly was Jesus saying by telling his story the way he did?

TELLING IT NORMAL: KEY ELEMENTS IN THE STORY

> 7 Then when Jesus noticed how the guests chose the places of honor, he told them a parable. He said to them, 8 "When you are invited by someone to a wedding feast, do not take the place of honor, because a person more distinguished than you may have been invited by your host. 9 So the host who invited both of you will come and say to you, 'Give this man your place.' Then, ashamed, you will begin to move to the least important place. 10 But when you are invited, go and take the least important place, so that when your host approaches he will say to you, 'Friend, move up here to a better place.' Then you will be honored in the presence of all who share the meal with you. 11 For everyone who exalts himself will be humbled, but the one who humbles himself will be exalted."
>
> 12 He said also to the man who had invited him, "When you host a dinner or a banquet, don't invite your friends or your brothers or your relatives or rich neighbors so you can be invited by them in return and get repaid. 13 But when you host an elaborate meal, invite the poor, the crippled, the lame, and the blind. 14 Then you will be blessed, because they cannot repay you, for you will be repaid at the resurrection of the righteous."

The complexity within an ancient banquet could create a large amount of confusion. There is however much more to this parable than eating. In those days, seating was an indicator of pecking order. The closer the guests sat to the host (who sat the farthest inside the house), the more honored the guests were. Jesus' parable in Luke 14:8–11 is based on the customs of hierarchical seating. Like today, there was probably some flexibility in lower rank table seating but the head table seating and the seats of honor were never in dispute in Jesus' day. In other words, only someone who had zero idea about social customs would pick the wrong seat. Yet, as I have explained above, picking seats in relation to others could be a confusing experience of walking on thin ice.

Based on the narrative in Luke 14:7, there were multiple seats to pick from. This is most likely the situation of a head table where guests would sit around this head table to eat. These desirable seats were closest to the host. Most likely, Jesus was talking about the seat at the right hand of the host in Luke 14:8, as an example. The parable has a strange plot. First, someone had mistakenly thought that he was more important than everyone else in Luke 14:8. Then, someone else more socially distinguished had come. Then, the original person who picked the seat of highest honor wasn't just moved away from the seat of honor, but was put in the least important seat in Luke 14:9.

Why would the man take the least important seat? Were there not other seats to be had? Sure, there were other seats to be had. The problem is that the man started out being the least important to begin with but assumed that he was the most important. Thus, Jesus was not saying that the confusion was between people of similar ranks but between two people of completely opposite ranks. The one who thought he was the most important but was actually least important had such a ridiculously inflated self esteem that he put himself in this awkward situation. Since the host would probably arrive late to the occasion and he knew where the host would sit (as was the custom in Jesus' day), he found the most important seat near the host. Ironically, his assumption landed him back into the least important seat. In other words, those who clamored for the best seats often overestimated their place and underestimated the place of others in their lives. This not just a little bit of overestimation. This was gross overestimation.

What would be the moral of this parable? Jesus gave the answer clearly in Luke 14:12–14. As expected, the answer has a good dose of eschatology, which links well to the next parable. Jesus told his listeners that if they did not assume they were better, but rather lowlier than others, they would certainly be honored. The principle of the kingdom was to humble self in order to be exalted. By humbling themselves, kingdom citizens would never grossly overestimate their abilities to their own embarrassing demise. Thus, kingdom citizens shouldn't assume honor. Rather, they ought to wait for assigned honor. With assigned honor, they will serve others the way Jesus served others.

CONTEXT

Within the context of the parable was the event in Luke 14:1–6. In Luke 14:3, Jesus made an aggressive ploy, bringing up the issue that was stated after the event in Luke 13:14. First, Jesus raised the problem of whether or not it was legal to heal on the Sabbath, a question already discussed on Luke 6:9. This silenced the Pharisees and the experts of the law in Luke 14:4. The Pharisees and experts of the law were indeed considered enemies of Jesus (cf. Luke 15:2). As a group, they had taken the lead in questioning Jesus. That was why Jesus addressed them in his inquiry. They had a gross overestimation of their own importance and a gross underestimation of the importance of others. The narrative does not elaborate on how Jesus healed the man because Luke's concern was no longer about the manner of the healing but about the timing and its implications for the faith community.

How in fact was this related to the parable? It is related in every single way. In the parable, those who were self-important were lowered and those who were lowly were lifted up. The very same thing happened in the healing event. The man who was suffering from illness was healed. The men who took charge of the religious settings and interpretation of the law were silenced by Jesus' questions and furthermore by his healing. Their silence in Luke 14:4–6 shows their rhetorical defeat. Most certainly, Jesus (and Luke also) wanted to bring the topic beyond Sabbath keeping to human dignity and hierarchy here. Since the audience was quiet, Jesus probed the question by talking about the value and dignity of human life in comparison to the animals in Luke 14:5, just as he did in Luke 13:15.

What did the parable have to do with the present situation of the banquet? Jesus had addressed the guests in Luke 14:7–11. Now in Luke 14:12–14, Jesus addressed the host, the same Pharisee who invited him in Luke 14:1. Why did Jesus need to address the host? It was due to the host's responsibility in the social ranking. Since the context of banqueting had to do with social status, Jesus was not talking about ordinary eating with a few friends. We shouldn't assume that Jesus was teaching that we should never invite friends over to eat.

The kind of banquet he talked about clearly had social and financial implications. Those who were invited desired to climb to the social place of the host. The hosts wanted to invite those they assumed to be of the same rank or of personal interest. The culture required those who were invited to reciprocate the favor (Luke 14:12). Luke 14:12 shows that Jesus was talking about both lunch and dinner. Since some in Jesus' day only ate two meals, these two meals symbolize all meals that had social implications. As favors were reciprocated repeatedly, the parties would cement the relationship and gain greater social power over others. That's the culture. The host looked for repayment. Yet, Jesus said to seek no repayment but to wait for God's repayment. In so doing, the host ought to invite those who were of no use to society or to himself, such as the poor and the handicap in Luke 14:13. Those who lacked the power to reciprocate would demonstrate God's power to reward. In essence, both the hosts and the guests had the same kingdom responsibility: they both needed to humble themselves. Jesus' teaching fit perfectly the social customs of his day. This teaching was not something from the ivory tower. It was something very practical. God would reward the humble and generous at the end. Thus, the person who had the inflated view of himself would be led to the lowest seat, per Luke 14:9. The lowly person in the same way would be exalted. Jesus told the parables to let them complement each other.

Yet, when we look at the whole healing situation, Jesus wasn't merely talking about eating, but he was talking about people, like the man he healed, who should be included in the earthly banquet all the time. That invitation to the poor would elevate their status and dignity. Jesus' healing was the expression of such a banquet. He wanted to elevate the lowly. Thus, the future of the believer's salvation ought to be expressed in the present social interaction with others. Earthly relationships ought to reflect future hope. Jesus' healing showed a glimpse of that future hope. In other words, the way these religious leaders reacted to the sick man indicated where they fit in the greater scheme of God's plan and the picture was not hopeful for them. They, like the person with the inflated view of himself, had an inflated view of their positions. Jesus deflated their views and exalted the lowly patient who was healed in Luke 14:4.

In context of the immediate narrative, we can say much more about the messianic banquet, but we'll talk about it in the next chapter.

PUTTING THE TEXT IN HISTORY: MEANINGS FOR THE WORLD OF AUTHOR-READERS

If Luke had been subtle about his message before, he wasn't now. Banqueting was an important part of social interaction and demonstration of social ranking. The invited guests were often those within one's social circles. Though the guests were sometimes higher or lower rank, they were always near the ranking of the host. People wouldn't invite others who were significantly lower rank to such a banquet.

Banqueting was also the luxury of the rich. Only very wealthy people had the facilities to host banquets, while the poorer majority barely had enough space to live. Some of the poor would be the slaves who worked within the household of the rich. They were there as subservient participants, mainly to serve the owner's needs. The relationship of banqueting was such that this group of relatively rich people would get together, and once someone invited a guest, the guest was then obligated to repay the kindness in some ways. If the guest had a big house, then hosting another banquet in the host's honor would be the right thing to do. Social customs dictated that the guest would always repay the host.

When we read Jesus' teachings, especially in Luke 14:13–14, it looks like a social nightmare for Theophilus. In Theophilus's world, these people Jesus said to invite were clearly invisible people. These disabled people were not contributors but burdens to society. They weren't ever esteemed to be honored guests. When Jesus said this, however, he said it in the context of the future hope. He said that God would repay the humble at the resurrection of the righteous (Luke 14:14). From Jesus' vantage point, this radical act of kindness wasn't just to disturb Theophilus's world, it was an act of faith and hope. Theophilus needed faith to believe that the righteous would indeed be resurrected. He also had hope that this would happen. Both faith and hope disturbed so much that Theophilus had to sacrifice his welfare in this life.

MODERN IMPLICATIONS

In the modern worldview, people find it hard to believe in the resurrection. Still, many Christians now claim that they believe in the resurrection. In fact, the resurrection is in many of our weekly creedal recitations during church. In reality though, many do not believe in the resurrection in the way they live their lives. Yet, Jesus appealed to that belief not in the abstract creedal and distant way of modern doctrines, but in a practical way.

The ways Christians handle relationships and wealth illustrate whether they live the resurrection faith. Jesus' suggestion is radical enough to shake our world, if we truly take it seriously. Jesus was talking about prioritizing those who are on the fringe over those who benefit us. We should think a bit about that. The irony of all ironies is that many in our world right now, even (especially) the progressives, are standing behind all sorts of causes in social justice while making a huge living off the same stance. While the original stance was admirable, a lot has gone off track. In this day and age of cyber stardom, anyone with or without qualifications can get famous, as long as the person plays the game right. A lot of financial gain can come from the game. Yet, Jesus despised the game. The game of huge repayment and benefits is not the kingdom. Jesus wanted the rich and those with privilege to abandon the game, not just to "speak for" the poor but to invite the poor into their lives. They weren't just to talk about the poor. They were to talk to the poor. They weren't just to speak about poor living conditions but were to invite the poor to better conditions that they could provide. This is extremely radical stuff. Most of us, if we're honest with ourselves, have fallen far short of what Jesus just talked about. Thus, in practice, many really don't act like they believe in the faith and hope of the resurrection.

Preachers who preach this sermon will have to do it at their own risk. This is an extremely inflammatory text in its context, content, and cultural background. There's no escaping its radical edge. As Jesus kept telling his parables, he certainly was sounding more and more radical. Instead of showing even a remote amount of respect to his host, he bluntly pointed out what was wrong with the banquet to which he was invited. Jesus was not one to show anyone respect here.

With the modern audience though, this sermon requires a readiness in the church, because if the lead pastors who preach aren't ready for that kind of radical change in church culture, they will end up sending out mixed signals to their listeners. Perhaps, the sermon can serve as the standard toward which the church can strive on its journey to live out the resurrection hope. The focal point really is whether people realize that they do things for benefits in the present life or for the resurrection life. The sermon ought to end with the same note, pointing to faith and hope the way Jesus did when he first told his parable. Integrity in this life is built on the present faith in the future hope.

REFLECTION QUESTIONS

1. What was so difficult about picking the right seat at an ancient banquet?
2. How did Jesus act impolitely in his attendance at this banquet?

Kingdom Faux Pas

3. What is the motivation for inviting the undesirables?
4. How did all this teaching challenge Theophilus?
5. In what way is this challenging to our modern church culture and our personal spiritual journeys?

9

The Impossible Rejection

TELLING IT BACKWARD: LUKE 14:15-24

> A man once gave a great banquet and invited many guests. At the time for the banquet he sent his slave to tell those who had been invited, "Come, because everything is now ready." Everyone came and enjoyed themselves at the master's table.

IN THE ANCIENT WORLD, turning down a banquet invitation was very bad manners. These days, some cultures still have such customs. Even in my own culture, those of my parents' generation simply don't turn down invitations to the weddings of one another's children. This is the Chinese way of maintaining a tight bond between relatives and even friends. My generation of Chinese-Americans tends to be less bound by such customs, but we also aren't as close in our networks as our parents' generation. At the same time, while my culture has this element in it, it doesn't always have the same financial implications as in Jesus' day. Then, most people simply didn't make excuses not to go. In fact, most excuses people give today would have been considered offensive. It is because in those days, those invited were dependent on the host. The host usually held all the power. As we have already stated earlier, those who could afford to host banquets were the rich who had the space in their houses to eat large meals. No one ought to offend the rich in that society. The story I tell above represents a normal relationship within the social customs of Jesus' day. Jesus told the story differently than above, but what exactly was Jesus saying by telling his story the way he did?

The Impossible Rejection

TELLING IT NORMAL: KEY ELEMENTS IN THE STORY

> 15 When one of those at the meal with Jesus heard this, he said to him, "Blessed is everyone who will feast in the kingdom of God!" 16 But Jesus said to him, "A man once gave a great banquet and invited many guests. 17 At the time for the banquet he sent his slave to tell those who had been invited, 'Come, because everything is now ready.' 18 But one after another they all began to make excuses. The first said to him, 'I have bought a field, and I must go out and see it. Please excuse me.' 19 Another said, 'I have bought five yoke of oxen, and I am going out to examine them. Please excuse me.' 20 Another said, 'I just got married, and I cannot come.' 21 So the slave came back and reported this to his master. Then the master of the household was furious and said to his slave, 'Go out quickly to the streets and alleys of the city, and bring in the poor, the crippled, the blind, and the lame.' 22 Then the slave said, 'Sir, what you instructed has been done, and there is still room.' 23 So the master said to his slave, 'Go out to the highways and country roads and urge people to come in, so that my house will be filled. 24 For I tell you, not one of those individuals who were invited will taste my banquet!'"

The story starts with a host inviting people to his banquet in Luke 14:16–17. This was not just any feast but a huge feast (implying a huge house), based on the humongous guest list the parable seems to indicate (Luke 14:22). Since one couldn't afford to offend such rich folks because they were the benefactors of the society, people would typically drop whatever they were doing to attend.

However, everyone unexpectedly made excuses not to go in Luke 14:18–20. The excuses ranged from having bought a field, to having bought some animals, to having gotten married. The order of field, oxen, and marriage is fascinating in that the excuses moved from financial to marital. The buying of a field came from the upper class of Jesus' day. The buying of oxen was due to the need to plow a large piece of land. While the excuses about purchases indicate wealth, marriage seems more basic. The excuses then would seem more and more reasonable from our modern perspective. But within ancient culture, the excuses made here were inexcusable. Why in fact would a new marriage have prevented someone from attending the banquet? None of the excuses had to do with life threatening situations. These were nonsensical excuses. Such is the folly of rejecting the banquet. Thus, the range of excuses went from the unreasonable to absurd, because the rejection of the messianic invitation is absurd. This parable then is a mockery against those who made excuses. They treated the banquet as if it were some kind of burdensome task.

The immediate result was not good in Luke 14:21 as the host, a powerful man, became angry. The host then sent his slave to invite more to come. No one was rushing to come into the banquet! Yet, this is reasonable because those who would have been invited, such as the guest list of underprivileged in Luke 14:22 would never think about attending. The places where the slave went in Luke 14:21 were probably where the outsiders hung out because the slaves found the down and out people. These were probably beggars who hung out in the alleys and streets. These underprivileged people would have been a stark contrast to the first two excuse makers. The ability to buy a field and five oxen shows that they were men of some wealth but they didn't go to the banquet. The Pharisee who hosted from Luke 14:1 could certainly have related to this degree of wealth. The poor would be the last invited and they became more like those who were first invited. This strange guest list is the same list Jesus used in Luke 14:13. Still there was room. So, the master told his slave to get people from all over to come in Luke 14:23. In fact, the language describing the invitation to these third-rate guests is quite forceful, depicting coercion for them to come in. Why? In a society where only people of similar rank would dine together, this was unheard of. More importantly, these poor folks would never be able to reciprocate the kindness shown by the host, a concept already clearly stated in Luke 14:13–14. These invitees were definitely the last of the last, and now their place in the kingdom had trumped those who were first invited.

When reading the parable with an understanding of the Pharisee as a host, it almost mimics what Jesus did with the Pharisee. In this way, the parable of the banquet functions like an allegory. Jesus acted as the host even though he was guest because he was the one who told the Pharisee to invite the underprivileged. The Pharisee then became the slave who had no choice but to invite those who were underprivileged. In doing so, he was merely doing what the master had asked him to do. It was not to be viewed as a burden but as obedience. In so doing, the slave would not fall into the fate of those who were invited but refused to come. In Jesus' story, the head Pharisee became the slave. At the same time, this parable taught the Pharisee to obey the previous parable as well, because the previous parable was about not overestimating one's own importance.

The Impossible Rejection

How in fact does this parable answer the question of whether healing on Sabbath was good? The answer to the question is, of course, "Yes." Not only should the sick man be healed on the Sabbath, but also the very idea of Sabbath should require the host to invite rejects such as this man to come and dine at the banquet. In this way, the Sabbath ought to reflect more of God's messianic banquet than glum religious prohibitions. In so doing, the rejected should be served as if they were the most important guests at the messianic banquet.

CONTEXT

When reading the parable, we have to remember that the entire parable occurred within the context of the event described in Luke 14:1–14. Jesus' parable of the banquet was a logical fit. Jesus ended the account with a parable when someone responded by talking about the feast at the kingdom of God in Luke 14:15, where the man called those who attend the feast "blessed" or the Greek word for "happy" in Luke 14:15. We can make it a more straightforward colloquial translation, "Whoever attends this feast would be so thrilled!" We should be quite aware that this story is also similar to the previous stories about banqueting in Luke's plot and will elaborate on Jesus' (or Luke's) emphasis in reading the story in light of preceding plot structure. They serve as twins to mirror each other for emphasis. Jesus responded with a story that also has a parallel in Matthew 22:1–14, only Luke's twice repeated theme of banqueting has a very practical, ethical, and literal dimension that isn't in Matthew.

It is important to note that the two analogies about the field and oxen put the emphasis on wealth because of the setting of the real banquet at which Jesus was eating. Such banquets were the occasion one shows off one's wealth and high society connections. All the excuses were of the same kind: they had other more important priorities. In an analogical way, those who didn't become disciples were disqualified not through the host's rejection, but through self-exclusion. They chose to despise the invitation. Does any of this answer the question of whether healing on the Sabbath was good? Sure, Jesus did indirectly reinforce the point of why the rejected received favors from the kingdom banquet. It is because they were the most helpless and most open to the blessings of the kingdom. Thus, this sick man personified those who were not in the mainstream of Judaism who would receive that blessing. The Sabbath was meant to draw such people to God.

Another perspective worth pondering is the way the present parable both imitates and contrasts with Luke 13:22–30 at the same time. While both parables sound like they are about entering through a house, Luke 13 is about people entering and Luke 14 is about people resisting invitation. More curious is that Luke 13 also has a Sabbath controversy just like here in Luke 14. To summarize, the plot line of the narrow door parable and this parable of the great banquet looks like this:

- Many do not bother to go in. (Luke 13:25; 14:16–20)
- The host has sovereignty. (Luke 13:25–27; 14:21–23)
- Those who go in are unexpected. (Luke 13:29–30; 14:21, 23)
- Those who are left out would miss the blessing and suffer for their neglect. (Luke 13:28; 14:24)

We should also be able to read Luke 14:15–24 as a variation of the previous parables. The Greek vocabulary for invitation is the same in Luke 14:8 and 14:16. This signals a similar scene as in the previous parables, but we shall see some variation as well. Similar to the previous two stories, Jesus introduced the address, though the vocabulary varies. Then, the parable starts with an invitation, but instead of the "don't . . . but when . . . you will" plot, Jesus focused on the refusal by those invited to attend at all, because they were distracted. So, the real banquet in Luke 14:7ff is viewed from the perspective of the host, while the banquet in the parable from Luke 14:16ff is viewed from the perspective of the guests. Finally, in Luke 14:21 the invitation was extended to a similar list as the one in Luke 14:13. At the end, this parable shows why the original guests shouldn't have been invited in the first place. An understanding of how the kingdom works inevitably ought to impact how the earthly host would treat others. It was God's kingdom value described in Luke 14:15–24 that gave even more reason for those listening to practice what was they had heard said in Luke 14:7–14. And if (as we just said regarding the Pharisee) the earthly host ought to think of himself as a slave to the true host, how much more ought he to reflect the true host's interests?

In summary, Jesus sounded like he was talking about the kingdom of God "out there" but he was really talking about the kingdom of God "among us." The way the kingdom would work on earth was through the banqueting action of the rich toward the poor. In so doing, the rich would reflect the will of the ultimate master in Jesus Christ. As strange as this sounds, the bizarre scenario of rejecting the master's banquet gives a richer meaning. For this strange scene suggests that if true kingdom citizens heard this story, they wouldn't reject its radical value system but would accept Jesus' strange idea on face value by obedience. Otherwise, they themselves had rejected the kingdom.

PUTTING THE TEXT IN HISTORY: MEANINGS FOR THE WORLD OF AUTHOR-READERS

As if the voluntary lowering of status in Luke 14:8 was not radical enough for Theophilus, Jesus' parable here surely took the idea of lowering oneself to the next level. Already, the previous parable talked about inviting the poor to come eat. That was the way to express the faith and hope for the resurrection. This parable took it one step further. This parable points out the importance of being part of the kingdom here and now, instead of expecting it to be something in the future.

Instead of enjoying the blessing of the kingdom, Theophilus would reflect the messianic banquet in his own banqueting habits. In other words, the way he ate and the company he kept became the gospel to others. Why indeed was this necessary? It was because Jesus wanted the kingdom citizen to express his lordship in the eating and drinking events of everyday relationships.

Theophilus wouldn't have missed the subversive message of this parable because during his time, there had been change of regimes and politicians. People like him depended on the good will of those with whom they associated. Yet, Jesus' parable declared the lordship of Jesus over all ruling powers, not by a victorious conquest of the regime but by serving the lowly within it. In so doing, the kingdom message triumphed in the ordinary everyday relationships.

MODERN IMPLICATIONS

Modern readers have often tried to recreate the kingdom of God in so many different ways. Some may start Christian communities by living in the same area together. Some others may do things like prayer walks so that God's reign might be seen in the neighborhood. While there's nothing inherently wrong with these activities, they don't fit what Jesus was saying or what Luke was saying to Theophilus. Still there are others who try to rigidly "obey God's law" (whatever that means) and create communities that follow certain rules. Although these aren't secluded monastic communities, they still do not necessarily have a big social impact. To many outsiders, this kind of kingdom expression just seems odd.

Jesus' solution is normal, productive, and radical all at once. Jesus insisted that believers ought to live their faith through their relationships. Their association with others should reflect God's heart in the kingdom. In so doing, they would reflect God's kingdom on earth. With the kingdom, there's always a king. The kingship of God doesn't come in the form of violent power but in service to the lowly. At the same time, believers shouldn't be surprised when others reject this value system, even though the parable suggested that such a rejection is absurd. While living out the radical vision seems absurd, Jesus deemed it normal. While living out the worldly value seems normal, Jesus deemed it absurd. The two are at war with one another.

The preacher who wishes to tackle this text must interpret this text based on understanding of context in Luke 14 as well as the similar scene in Luke 13. Matthew 22 has a different context, and mustn't be mixed into this rich narrative of Luke. Matthew stressed the coming of the Son of Man. Luke had a much more social message about the here and now. To have a contextual interpretation doesn't mean that the preacher has to cover the entire text of Luke 13–14 to be faithful in the preaching this parable. Preachers who consider the surrounding context will find quickly that the parable is not about God's kingdom "out there." Instead, preachers should preach the parable as an exemplary story about how we as believers should function in real-world relationships. This, too, will challenge the way the church reads the messianic feast exclusively in terms of the future. Preachers ought to assert that Jesus really wanted his listeners to take this parable as an example of how the church should function in this world to create messianic feasts here and now.

REFLECTION QUESTIONS

1. What does the different retelling of the story reflect?
2. Why did Jesus choose those excuses to show rejection?
3. What implications are there when we link this parable with the previous setting?

4. What implications are there when we link it to the previous Sabbath controversy and the parable in Luke 13?
5. How do we see that the kingdom is not "out there" in this parable?
6. How should the kingdom be expressed in today's world?

10

The Lost Son?

TELLING IT DIFFERENT: LUKE 15

A man had two sons. The younger of them said to his father, "Father, give me the share of the estate that will belong to me." So he divided his assets between them. After a few days, the younger son gathered together all he had and left on a journey to a distant country, and there he squandered his wealth with a wild lifestyle. Then after he had spent everything, a severe famine took place in that country, and he began to be in need. So he went and worked for one of the citizens of that country, who sent him to his fields to feed pigs. He was longing to eat the carob pods the pigs were eating, but no one gave him anything. But when he came to his senses he said, "How many of my father's hired workers have food enough to spare, but here I am dying from hunger! I will get up and go to my father and say to him, 'Father, I have sinned against heaven and against you. I am no longer worthy to be called your son; treat me like one of your hired workers.'" So he got up and went to his father. But while he was still a long way from home his father saw him, and his heart went out to him; he ran and hugged his son and kissed him. Then his son said to him, "Father, I have sinned against heaven and against you; I am no longer worthy to be called your son." But the father said to his slaves, "Hurry! Bring the best robe, and put it on him! Put a ring on his finger and sandals on his feet! Bring the fattened calf and kill it! Let us eat and celebrate, because this son of mine was dead, and is alive again—he was lost and is found!" So they began to celebrate.

The Lost Son?

THIS IS A FUN story. Preachers have preached it to death, or at least authors have written innumerable words on it through the ages. The above retelling shows a much more popular interpretation by both preachers and writers. This retelling focuses on the young son as the lost son. Indeed, most sermons make the older son a footnote. If this footnote gets mentioned at all, the preacher often points a self-righteous finger at the work-oriented Pharisee or Jew.

Without any doubt, the popular interpretation of the parable is at least half right. The younger son was lost in several ways. First, he wanted to get his inheritance before his father died. At the very least, his request wouldn't fit the social convention of how people handled inheritance. The younger son betrayed his own folly in his request, leading to further questionable choices. He certainly wasted no time in spending what he didn't earn. Second, he squandered what he inherited and put himself at a great social risk with no safety net. He was essentially depending on his brother's good will (who controlled the remainder of the family assets) and obviously, his brother didn't have any good will toward him, but we shall talk about that later. Third, his desperation worsened as the land suffered famine and he had no money. Thus, not only his own habit had failed him, but nature also failed him. Fourth, he even sank so low as to want to eat defiled food. Dietary scruples don't matter when one is starving. Fifth, he schemed in his mind about how to talk to his father based on his own value system of trespass and repercussion. Finally, he went home.

When the son returned home, the father felt compassion toward him and he ran to hug and kiss him, even in his disgusting state. Instead of letting the son finish his rehearsed sentence, the father hurriedly ordered his slaves to clean up the son and have a banquet in his honor. This story has a happy ending with the son coming home. However, Jesus told the story differently than above, but what exactly was Jesus saying by telling his story the way he did?

TELLING IT NORMAL: KEY ELEMENTS IN THE STORY

> 11 A man had two sons. 12 The younger of them said to his father, "Father, give me the share of the estate that will belong to me." So he divided his assets between them. 13 After a few days, the younger son gathered together all he had and left on a journey to a distant country, and there he squandered his wealth with a wild

lifestyle. 14 Then after he had spent everything, a severe famine took place in that country, and he began to be in need. 15 So he went and worked for one of the citizens of that country, who sent him to his fields to feed pigs. 16 He was longing to eat the carob pods the pigs were eating, but no one gave him anything. 17 But when he came to his senses he said, "How many of my father's hired workers have food enough to spare, but here I am dying from hunger! 18 I will get up and go to my father and say to him, 'Father, I have sinned against heaven and against you. 19 I am no longer worthy to be called your son; treat me like one of your hired workers.'" 20 So he got up and went to his father. But while he was still a long way from home his father saw him, and his heart went out to him; he ran and hugged his son and kissed him. 21 Then his son said to him, "Father, I have sinned against heaven and against you; I am no longer worthy to be called your son." 22 But the father said to his slaves, "Hurry! Bring the best robe, and put it on him! Put a ring on his finger and sandals on his feet! 23 Bring the fattened calf and kill it! Let us eat and celebrate, 24 because this son of mine was dead, and is alive again—he was lost and is found!" So they began to celebrate.

25 Now his older son was in the field. As he came and approached the house, he heard music and dancing. 26 So he called one of the slaves and asked what was happening. 27 The slave replied, "Your brother has returned, and your father has killed the fattened calf because he got his son back safe and sound." 28 But the older son became angry and refused to go in. His father came out and appealed to him, 29 but he answered his father, "Look! These many years I have worked like a slave for you, and I never disobeyed your commands. Yet you never gave me even a goat so that I could celebrate with my friends! 30 But when this son of yours came back, who has devoured your assets with prostitutes, you killed the fattened calf for him!" 31 Then the father said to him, "Son, you are always with me, and everything that belongs to me is yours. 32 It was appropriate to celebrate and be glad, for your brother was dead, and is alive; he was lost and is found."

The story is very straightforward when we add the elder son into the mix. Without the elder son, the return of the younger son was the climax. With the return of the elder son, the elder son's conversation with his father becomes the climax. The content of the elder son's objection is interesting in that he filled in the blanks of what the narrator, Jesus, failed to mention. In Luke 15:13–14, while Jesus said that the younger son spent everything he had on wild living, he didn't catalogue the nature of wild living. In Luke

15:30, the elder son specifically stated that the younger son had spent all the money on prostitutes. This active imagination of the elder son speaks volumes of what he thought about his younger brother. Certainly, he wasn't present when his younger brother was doing his dirty deeds, but perhaps he wasn't far wrong. When people have a judgmental attitude, they always imagine the worst about others. Neither the narrator Jesus nor the father accounted for the sins. Grace doesn't take an account of every trespass. Thus, the elder son provided a contrast to both the attitude of Jesus and that of the father. The parable itself illustrates the stark contrast between grace and judgment.

When reading this story, it is important not to see Jesus laying out some kind of new divine compassion that didn't exist in the Old Testament. This story is not about the contrast between the New Testament grace against the Old Testament judgment. Jesus' point is that grace had always been at the heart of God's will. The parable was Jesus' means to remind his audience of this forgotten truth. The parable also doesn't discount the sinful lifestyle of the son. The parable is realistic. It isn't some kind of rose-colored painting where all sins are dismissed. The father's compassion that led to his joy allowed him to overlook realistic trespasses.

CONTEXT

The context of this parable comes in three layers. The first layer comes in Luke 14:25–35. The location for this event is the way to Jerusalem, according to Luke 14:25. More importantly, during this actual journey Jesus talked about the metaphorical journey of following him. In a sense, for Luke, this narrative journey acts as a parable of what it meant to follow Jesus. The second layer is the narrative structure that is linked with the stories before the story of the lost son. The third layer, of course, is in Luke 15:1–2 where the religious leaders mumbled about what Jesus did with sinners, probably including the tax collectors of Luke 15:1.

What can we gather from the first layer? The occasion shows that many were following Jesus in Luke 14:25. Instead of waiting for people to say that they wanted to follow Jesus, Jesus talked about the harsh criteria for following him: to hate both family members and life itself (Luke 14:26) and then to carry one's cross to one's own death (Luke 14:27). The occasion was meant to deter followers from following Jesus too easily. Of course, Jesus wasn't talking about a literal hatred of the household, but was talking hyperbolically about prioritizing discipleship so much that in comparison, even the most basic household relationship would look like hatred, the very opposite of love. Jesus' teaching was also extremely subversive to his own society. It would upset the entire Empire because the household was the metaphor also for the empire with the head of household being the Caesar. Jesus continued with a two analogies to explain why he said what he said.

The first analogy in Luke 14:28–30 is architectural. The analogy is simple. Someone decided to build a tower to protect his farmland or his town but failed to account for its cost. At the end, this person laid the foundation without having much success building on top of it. His final result was ridicule from all those who passed by. The second analogy in Luke 14:31–33 is imperial. One king decided to war against another king. Upon closer evaluation of the available manpower, the initiator of the attack realized that his manpower was only half of his opponent's. The smart thing to do was to send a delegation out to make peace before the opposing army got too close to attack. Jesus' final conclusion in Luke 14:33 is curious, though. He didn't say to make peace in the same way, but he said that in the same way, the calculation needed to be made when following him, and that calculation was to give up everything. In the two analogies, Jesus gave the perfect setting for the occasion for this series of parables. A lot of people have not thought through their situation and the cost of following Jesus before following Jesus, much like the incompetent fools in the analogies. What exactly was the cost however? The answer will come in the next layer of context.

The second layer is the framework from which Jesus told the story of the lost son. The framework comes from Luke 15:3–10. This framework can be taken for granted but the obvious elements aren't in the details. First of all, Luke said that Jesus was telling a single "parable" in Luke 15:3. Many experts still want to see the entire chapter as three parables. While there may be some hints of the three stories being three parables, there was really no break in Jesus' speech. Neither was there any change in audience or occasion. It is better to see the chapter as one gigantic parable with three stories or three parts. Common to this entire framework are the words or themes "lost . . . found . . . rejoice" (Luke 15:4–7, 8–10, 24, 32). Many derive a lot of meaning from the lost coin and lost sheep stories, seeing a progression from dead coin to living sheep and finally to the son. Most likely, the lost coin and sheep serve as the introductory framework to the lost son story by introducing the pattern of lost, found, and celebration. Certainly, Luke 15:24 confirms this is the case.

The framework of the introductory stories of coin and sheep sets up the lost son story in a big way. The lost son story certainly can speak of the analogical love of God for sinners as stated earlier in Luke 15:7, 10. Yet, we can press the analogy too far. The outstanding segment is the part about the elder son that breaks the pattern of lost, found, and rejoice. By the outline of the coin and sheep stories, the lost son story ought to end nicely at Luke 15:24, but then there is the odd section about the elder son. The real ending is Luke 15:31–32, where the father restated the theme of lost, found, and being glad. In other words, Jesus didn't just highlight the love of father but the anger of the elder son. The elder son became the climax of the story.

While the younger brother had already gone inside, now the elder son lingered outside when Jesus ended the story. Would he go in? He certainly had potential to go in because all that the father had was his (Luke 15:31). Still, he had to enter in order to enjoy what was his. The emphasis of the conversation also points to the relationship between the three characters: the father, the younger son, and the elder son. The elder son who rejected his younger brother called him "this son of yours" in Luke 15:30. The father, however, called the younger brother "this brother of yours" in Luke 15:32. Jesus focused on relationship and not trespasses. In the story, the elder son was the true prodigal, as he didn't understand how his father or the household worked. He hadn't entered at the end while his "found" brother did enter.

Now that the second layer has become part of our framework, we should also look at the third layer of the narrative in the company Jesus kept. In many ways, this is an important part of the framework to clarify whether the reading above is accurate or not. The third framework comes in Luke 15:1–2. Jesus was hanging about with tax collectors and sinners, and the religious leaders were mumbling about the company Jesus kept. In many ways, Jesus' parable directly addressed their objection by saying that they were more like the older brother. While the younger brother was a sinner, he was loved because the father considered him as part of the family. However, the older brother didn't get this relationship, thus causing him to be the real prodigal son. The parable served to condemn the religious leaders to be most like the elder son.

How do we summarize what the contextual reading of the parable is? Since Luke framed the parable within Jesus' travel to Jerusalem, he was saying that part of the cost of discipleship and self-sacrifice involved proper understanding of relationships. Not only did the closest kin become someone the disciples left behind, but also the furthest stranger, the sinner, would become the disciples' brother. This apparently is part of the cost of being a disciple. Such is the ironic ethics of Luke. Within the framework of Jesus' setting, we learn that while the parable might teach about God's love for the sinner, it teaches the absurdity of spite toward sinners. It's as absurd as refusing to enter one's own house simply because of hatred, exemplified in the way the elder son behaved. While the first two stories of lost coin and lost sheep call for identification with those who have lost things, the last story both calls for identification with the father's sentiments, and denies the legitimacy of the elder son's attitude.

PUTTING THE TEXT IN HISTORY: MEANINGS FOR THE WORLD OF AUTHOR-READERS

This long story so far would have been quite the lesson for Theophilus. Luke continued to subvert Theophilus's world. Here, unexpectedly, following Jesus meant to abandon not just the banqueting tradition, but one's whole life. By social standards, the only reason Theophilus ought to consider losing his life would be for the sake of Rome. Now, Jesus clearly pointed out that losing one's life was part of following him. Luke's writing however wasn't trying to teach Theophilus that Judaism was inherently bad or graceless. It was more about having compassion that would lead to joy over those who were unlikely members of God's household.

Theophilus would find the teaching subversive in that it propelled him to adopt not only those who were undesirable in Luke 14, but also those he might even despise in Luke 15. After all, the elder son despised his brother for good reasons. Luke was not denying the fact that certain people were despicable sinners. They weren't only social outcasts. They were outright sinners who had done serious wrongs. Theophilus was to keep company with them and reject the attitude of the religious leaders in the story.

It is important to note that Luke was not teaching an anti-Semitic lesson by depicting the religious leaders as absolutely evil. Judaism wasn't the modern Taliban or the Islamic State. Certainly, total condemnation of Judaism would have been a gross overstatement. After all, the religious leaders' attitude, if typified in the elder son's sentiments, did belong to the household. Both Luke and Jesus were much more subtle. They merely pointed out the fact that people like the religious leaders couldn't enjoy the benefit of the household because of their spite. Theophilus must learn to enjoy the blessing he had received through his faith by freely granting grace to the undeserving. Theophilus wasn't just to tolerate these sinners; he was to rejoice. Grace then was not a transaction to be traded for other favors. Theophilus was to give grace freely even to those who had done nothing to deserve it. Like the little brother, those who had squandered everything had no ability to repay anyone. In fact, like the little brother, they would have been reliant on the good will of the elder brother. The proper elder brother would use what he now had, which was everything that the father had, and share with the undeserving younger brother. It's one thing to help the poor as charity case, but it's quite another to love a delinquent brother.

MODERN IMPLICATIONS

The parable is a great analogy for modern relationships. Modern relationships can be so convenient. Facebook has become a microcosm or even a caricature of those relationships. The button "like" carries a lot of implications. People like things for all different reasons. A while back, the "like" button actually caused one to have to follow a certain thread. Now, the new "like" button is only a "like" but doesn't make users follow the thread unless they also leave a comment. The number of likes can then increase due to the convenience of this feature. Furthermore, people can now stop following a certain thread, especially when certain despicable people show up to comment. These functions fix what we can't have in real-life relationships.

In real-life relationships, we can't easily walk away from something we say that we like or dislike. If we like a certain cause, we're forced to commit to it. If we hate other causes, we may not always be able to walk away either. Moreover, we can't simply stop following certain relationships unless we detach ourselves from their social settings. We don't always live as individuals. We live in community. Within a community context, in order to avoid conflicts, we tend to deal with one another as if nothing is wrong. This is naively noble, but unrealistic. Neither Luke nor Jesus denied that the younger brother was despicable. The parable graciously tells the brutal and honest truth. The challenge of modern relationships is that sometimes we think grace is best served by not telling the whole truth because we have trouble telling straight truth graciously. The parable reminds modern readers that truth about sin is best served with grace.

The best way to view this gracious truth telling is to look at relationships in terms of the kingdom. Jesus didn't demand harsh judgment in the kingdom. Jesus demanded that we put down our sense of justice to let grace triumph over our self-righteousness. Jesus wasn't saying that there's no standard for right and wrong. However, relationships in the kingdom aren't merely about score keeping. They are about giving freely to those in need of grace. Sometimes, the worst sinners need the most grace, illustrated in what Jesus had taught in Luke 7:36–43. To rejoice in the lost and found younger son required the father to see the son as having intrinsic value simply because he was his son. To rejoice takes a completely different perspective. The younger son is not a charity project. The younger son is a most valued member of the community worthy of an extravagant banquet.

The modern preacher faces the challenge of tradition here again. The popular reading of the parable puts the focus on the younger son and even the grace of God. Essentially, the popular interpretation often does away with the older son altogether. Many preachers tell the story differently than I did above, but that wasn't the story Jesus told. If we want to focus on God's grace, the first two stories of the lost coin and lost sheep already make it quite clear that God is gracious toward sinners. To say it once more makes little difference. While Jesus didn't deny God's grace, the message of Jesus in the lost son story put the focus on the older son. Now I'm not saying that the popular reading is unfounded, but the climactic emphasis should land squarely on those who are gracelessly self-righteous.

Another homiletical pitfall preachers must avoid is the inadvertent anti-Semitic reading of this parable. It's easy to celebrate that we aren't the "self-righteous Pharisees of Judaism." It's even easier to point finger at others. In applying Jesus' teaching here, the prayer "thank God I'm not a self-righteous Pharisee" isn't an option. The parable isn't trying to create even a greater self-righteous attitude. Rather, it is a mirror to examine each of our faith communities to see if we can truly rejoice in our embracing of erring younger sons, or whether we merely tolerate them at best and see them as our marginalized projects at worst.

This sermon will be difficult to preach because the cultures of many faith communities are indeed self-righteous. The entrenched anti-Semitic, self-righteous reading doesn't help at all. People tend to celebrate how good and moral they are rather than how much love they are to show to the seemingly undeserving. People want to see others as the lost son without wanting to see themselves as the elder son. Each community will face a

The Lost Son?

different challenge of self-righteousness. It's up to ministers to draw the proper analogy within their own ministries to make this parable not just something about sinners needing Jesus, but the righteous needing the compassion of the father.

REFLECTION QUESTIONS

1. What is the popular interpretation of this parable?
2. Why is it more important to read the story as part of a greater parable?
3. How do the coin and sheep stories preface the son story?
4. What is the focal point of the story?
5. How does this story fit with Jesus' teachings about following him?

11

What's Wrong with Being Rich?

TELLING IT DIFFERENT: LUKE 16:14-31

> There was a rich man who dressed in purple and fine linen and who feasted sumptuously every day. But at his gate lay a poor man named Lazarus whose body was covered with sores, who longed to eat what fell from the rich man's table. In addition, the dogs came and licked his sores. Therefore the rich man gave alms, as a good Jew would, to Lazarus to alleviate his suffering. After he died, both the rich man and Lazarus sat at the table with Abraham because they both were children of Abraham who belonged to different social classes in their earthly lives.

THE ABOVE STORY WOULD be different than the one Jesus told because the rich man did his duty and ended up in the same place as Lazarus. The real climax of Jesus' story was the eternal fate of the characters. That's why I changed the outcome, but the outcome obviously was due to the original lives both men lived.

When reading the story, it is quite easy for modern readers to pass judgment, but in reality, it would have been difficult for the rich man to detect the need of the invisible Lazarus. In Jesus' day, poverty was commonplace. The rich were quite filthy rich and the poor were extremely poor. The middle class, as we know it today, probably didn't exist. People from different social and economic classes did not cross over to each other's worlds. Unless someone heeded what Jesus said to the rich young ruler in Luke 12:32 to sell all that he had and give it to the poor, the rich would never descend to the level of the poor. In that society, the best a decent rich person could do was to give alms to the poor to help feed them. Almsgiving was commonplace in Judaism. However, Jesus told the story with no mention of almsgiving and strikingly without any mention of God, but what exactly was Jesus saying by telling his story the way he did?

TELLING IT NORMAL: KEY ELEMENTS IN THE STORY

> 19 There was a rich man who dressed in purple and fine linen and who feasted sumptuously every day. 20 But at his gate lay a poor man named Lazarus whose body was covered with sores, 21 who longed to eat what fell from the rich man's table. In addition, the dogs came and licked his sores.
>
> 22 Now the poor man died and was carried by the angels to Abraham's side. The rich man also died and was buried. 23 And in hell, as he was in torment, he looked up and saw Abraham far off with Lazarus at his side. 24 So he called out, "Father Abraham, have mercy on me, and send Lazarus to dip the tip of his finger in water and cool my tongue, because I am in anguish in this fire." 25 But Abraham said, "Child, remember that in your lifetime you received your good things and Lazarus likewise bad things, but now he is comforted here and you are in anguish. 26 Besides all this, a great chasm has been fixed between us, so that those who want to cross over from here to you cannot do so, and no one can cross from there to us." 27 So the rich man said, "Then I beg you, father—send Lazarus to my father's house 28 (for I have five brothers) to warn them so that they don't come into this place of torment." 29 But Abraham said, "They have Moses and the prophets; they must respond to them." 30 Then the rich man said, "No, father Abraham, but if someone from the dead goes to them, they will repent." 31 He replied to him, "If they do not respond to Moses and the prophets, they will not be convinced even if someone rises from the dead."

Is this story about the afterlife? Clearly, it is. If this story weren't about the afterlife, Jesus wouldn't have told it in this fashion. Yet, is this story about the every detail of the afterlife? Probably not. Jesus was not trying to teach, "This is what your afterlife will be like." Jesus told this as a parable, a kind of fiction through creative thinking, to illustrate his message.

Many who read this story think that in the days of Jesus, wealth was an indicator of divine blessing and poverty was a curse. This wasn't necessarily true for this story and, certainly, this logic would curse most of the population because most of the population was made up of ordinary poor folks.

This is an almsgiving story, if we consider the social situation of Jewish piety that would extend into the church community later.

The plot of the story is straightforward. Right away, Jesus said that the man was dressed in purple in Luke 16:19. Generally, a lot of the Roman officials dressed in purple, but later verses say that he was someone who kept calling Abraham father (e.g., Luke 16:24, 27, 31) and Abraham acknowledged that he was indeed one of his children (e.g., Luke 16:25). Not a lot of Jews were involved in the Roman government in an official capacity because of a lot of pagan practices ran counter to Jewish sensibilities. This official was probably a proselyte at the synagogue with a Gentile background, who was also considered to be a "son of Abraham." He was obviously very extravagant in his living, evident by the way Luke 16:19 describes him. All the while, the beggar Lazarus had nothing other than scraps of garbage to eat outside the rich man's gate where his slave probably threw leftover food from under his table (Luke 16:21).

As we examine the vocabulary describing Lazarus, we can tell that he's in a lowly place. Lazarus's lowly place comes from the word "lay" at Luke 16:20. The Greek actually means "was laid." In other words, someone laid him there. Lazarus was probably so crippled that someone put him there like a piece of rubbish to beg. The gate symbolized the chasm between the rich and the poor. The gate kept out all the riff raff and other undesirables like Lazarus. Sadly, even though Lazarus's name, in its Hebrew form, actually means, "God has helped," he's about as helpless as a statue. Noteworthy is the naming of Lazarus and the namelessness of the rich man. The only descriptive characteristics of this man were his wealth and extravagance. People only knew him by his social status and possessions. However, his name being left out was an ominous sign for Jesus' listeners. What picture had Jesus painted so far about the rich man? The rich man was callously rich. He ignored Lazarus who was at his gate and treated him as invisible. He further flaunted his wealth in the face of social poverty that was even at his gate. He had zero compassion. Like the rich fool in Luke 12:13–21, God didn't play a role in the story about his lifetime.

After death, they experienced a reversal of fortune. The location of Lazarus's eternal abode was geographically higher than the rich man's. Surely, in his lifetime, the rich man's social status was higher, but in eternity, classification reverses by their eternal locations. Lazarus, who was carried like a piece of rubbish in this life, was carried by angels to his eternal abode (Luke 16:22). On the contrary, the rich man was just "buried" in Luke

What's Wrong with Being Rich?

16:22. Although Lazarus had a name, he functioned more as a foil for Jesus' listeners because he was completely mute in the story. The main conversation was between Abraham and the rich man.

Many Christian readers would speculate as to why Lazarus was in this eternal abode. We may never know why Lazarus was in the eternal abode. Modern readers with a Christian background might ask why, but the story doesn't say, and there's no reason to focus on what's absent in the story. Jesus gave more important details here: Lazarus's posture of being by Abraham's side. This was like the paternal picture of a father holding a child. Yet, we can't help but wonder if Abraham was dining with Lazarus, for ancient people dined reclining sideways toward one another. The comment about getting some drinkable water for the rich man in Luke 16:24 further affirms the dining image.

In Jesus' narration, Abraham in his conversation with the rich man was eager to point out the irony. In this life, poor Lazarus was barely able to eat the rich man's scraps because the dogs were competing (Luke 16:21). In the next life, the rich man begged only for water because food was too extravagant (Luke 16:23). In this life, the rich man was dining (Luke 16:25). In the next, poor Lazarus would dine. In this life, the obstacle was the gate (Luke 16:20). In the next, the chasm between Abraham and Hades (or as some translations call it "hell") would be impossible to cross (Luke 16:26).[1] In this life, the rich man treated Lazarus as invisible. In the next, he would ask Abraham to send Lazarus as if Lazarus was the ambassador between the eternal abode and hell (Luke 16:27). Throughout all this, the rich man didn't quite get the point. He still acted like he could order Lazarus to save his own family simply because he was rich. Abraham would have none of that.

Instead of giving in to the rich man's demand, Abraham simply answered the rich man in Luke 16:29 that the rich man's family had the entire Bible (i.e., "Moses and the Prophets"). In other words, Jesus' teaching didn't bring anything new. The idea of compassion for the poor had always been in the teachings of the Bible. If the rich man's family were even remotely familiar with the Bible, they would know that this teaching filled many parts of the holy writings. Abraham further told the rich man that it would be useless to send a resurrected Lazarus to the rich family if the family didn't obey the Bible. Realistically, if the rich man's family were just like him, why would they listen to a resurrected beggar? Rich people like them simple

---

1. It is hard to translate the word for "hell" because in Greek myths it is the word "Hades," where the miserable dead continued to live their afterlives.

wouldn't listen to beggars in any way, shape, or form. If they did listen to Moses and the Prophets, they would've noticed poor Lazarus before he died. If Lazarus were invisible to them, what would make the resurrected Lazarus any more visible? Abraham's emphasis was not the ignorance but the knowledge of the family. Especially helpful is the description of their need to respond. In this parable, knowing was not enough. Deeds demonstrate true knowledge.

CONTEXT

The context of this parable begins in Luke 16:1–18 as the closest structural perimeter, but really, it should go all the way back to Luke 14:25. We should first consider the impact of the passage just prior in Luke 16 briefly on our interpretation. Then, we can look at how the passages from Luke 14–15 contribute to the present parable to derive the whole meaning of the event.

The section Luke 16:1–9 tells the parable that precedes the story of the rich man and Lazarus. I haven't dealt with the parable of the shrewd manager because I've already written about it elsewhere.[2] Hoping not to repeat too much of what I wrote in my previous work, I ought to deal with some of the unique feature of the shrewd manager story so that we can link up the story with the rich man and Lazarus story.

In Luke 16:1, Jesus told the story to the disciples about a wasteful manager. In a Roman household, the manager's job was to make sure resources were distributed evenly and invested wisely. This manager was probably a hired hand instead of a slave because he was sacked from his job. This manager's problem progressed from bad to worse as the manager got fired in Luke 16:2. His response was to come up with a solution in Luke 16:3–7 by cutting the debts of those who owed his master, most likely behind his master's back until it was too late for his master to undo the damage. The debts were owed in olive oil (Luke 16:6) and wheat (Luke 16:7). The amount of money owed was so astronomical that it would have taken ten years for the greatest debtor to pay it back. The reason why the debt came in the form of agricultural produce is unclear, as tenant farmers didn't have enough land to owe this much to the owner or to hire the manager.

Jesus basically told the parable in an exaggerated fictitious form. Several features are worthy of note. First, the manager made the debtors rewrite their own debt, thus, putting the responsibility on the debtors on the one hand,

2. Tsang, *Right Texts*, 62–71.

while putting them in his debt on the other. Second, by logical deduction, if he represented the master in pardoning the debtors partially, he had just made the master look like a generous person. Instead of getting a scolding from an angry master, the manager actually received praise for his shrewdness in Luke 16:8. Jesus declared the manager's value to have come from "people of this world" in Luke 16:8b, because they made their decision based on the values of this world that had not yet been redeemed by Jesus' work. Jesus was demonstrating that people of this world were able to handle the problems of this world better than his followers, who did far worse with the problems of the redeemed world. What value was Jesus referring to? Jesus provided a specific explanation in Luke 16:8–13. Jesus' explanation can be quite puzzling. Therefore, we should look closely at what he did say and what he didn't say. Jesus had more negative than positive lessons in this parable.

Initially, Jesus affirmed the positive lesson from the parable. Luke 16:8b–9 points to the importance of relationship over money. How was the manager shrewd? He was shrewd because he used his master's money to build up relationships. Jesus used the manager to reflect the positive usage of money to gain relationships. Negatively, Jesus literally called the money "unrighteous" instead of the usual translation of "worldly" in Luke 16:9. How so? Jesus was not advocating the use of dishonest financial means to gain friends. The wealth was unrighteous because the way the manager used it was unrighteous. He didn't represent his master well. He was not a good manager and he deserved to be sacked. The present example of how he abused his master's money is a perfect example of his questionable practices. Surely, Jesus wasn't advocating for his disciples to serve God by misusing resources and losing investments.

Luke's storytelling has an even more sophisticated plot structure when we read Luke 16:1–9 in light of the younger son's story in Luke 15:11–32. This manager, according to the way Jesus told the story, behaved much like the bad younger son. The double usage of "squander" in Luke 15:13 and Luke 16:1 hints at the parallel. The structure would look something like this:

squandering[3]	Luke 15:11–13	Luke 16:1
consequences	Luke 15:14–16	Luke 16:2
conversation with self	Luke 15:17–20	Luke 16:3–4
execution and success	Luke 15:20b–24	Luke 16:5–8a
teaching on relationship	Luke 15:25–32	Luke 16:8b–9

3. The words for "squander" and "waste" are the same in Greek.

Right Parables, Wrong Perspectives

The parable resulted in Pharisees sneering at Jesus in Luke 16:14, which led Jesus to condemn their love of money. The connection between this part and the other parts in Luke 16:16–18 can be difficult to interpret. So far, we can say that Jesus positively affirmed that money ought to be invested in building relationships that benefit the long term, and that involved not serving money. Jesus also affirmed that the manager wasn't a good manager. His entire way of doing things wasn't worthy of imitation.

How then does this parable of the manager fit with the rich man and Lazarus? The commendable trait of the manager was his ability to see the importance of relationship for the future. Money was the means by which he would build that future. The rich man had money, but had no future. His story became a warning to Jesus' listeners. They were to heed the warning and invest not in possessions or personal indulgence but in meaningful relationships.

Jesus now provided the introduction to the next parable in Luke 16:16–18. This is a difficult section, and many scholars try to find a theological solution here to explain the seemingly disjointed saying that precedes the parable. Luke 16:16 is not as difficult to interpret if we keep in mind the entire event beginning at Luke 14:1. Luke 14:23 clearly shows that many were entering the kingdom and Luke 16:16 only confirms that crowded membership. The statement about divorce however in connection to the permanence of the law is difficult.

We must keep in mind that this transitional introduction is Jesus' way of answering the Pharisees' love for money, just like the parable of the rich man and Lazarus, and the interpretation would be readily obvious. In Jesus' day, a certificate of divorce was allowed in order to give permission for remarriage. Although the law allowed divorce (Deut 24:1–4), the original marriage would still be considered permanent in the definition of God's Law.

Why did Jesus use marriage to illustrate the permanence of the Law? It is because marriage was about the most basic human relationship and the previous parable talks about relationship in Luke 16:9. This transitional section isn't trying to teach about marriage and divorce. Neither is it trying to allegorize the general permanence of the Law being like a marriage. Jesus only used the topic of marriage to illustrate the importance of relationship in God's law. The relationship part is the indicator of the ongoing function of the Torah. The permanence of the Law is its relational aspect, as the next rich man and Lazarus story would fully illustrate.

What's Wrong with Being Rich?

We should now look at how the story of the rich man and Lazarus links up with the above transitional point. The story of the rich man and Lazarus ends with great coherence. It ties back to Luke 16:16 where Jesus mentioned the Law and the Prophets. As we have said before, the Law and the Prophets were mentioned along with the divorce so that the idea of valuing relationship above everything would dominate. Moses and the Prophets in Luke 16:31 ended the story to show the consistent theme of the whole of Scripture addressing the importance of relationship. Yet, the definition of relationship was unclear in earlier discussion because the previous parable didn't really give a clear idea of what relationship Jesus was talking about until the parable of the rich man and Lazarus. Thus, the relationship Jesus was talking about had to do with the wealth disparity between the rich and the poor in the patron-client relationship. Already, the rich man should've known about Deuteronomy 14:28–29; 15:1–3, 7–15; etc., and how relationship with the poor was part of the Torah's core values.

What can we infer from the context surrounding the story about the rich man and Lazarus? To summarize, Jesus valued relationships over money in his kingdom. The specific kind of relationship comes out of the story about the rich man and Lazarus. Monetary investment should be directed to the poor like Lazarus. Those who were rich should care for the poor because the way the disciples handled that relationship in the here and now would impact their future. Jesus was not against the rich. He was against a callous attitude some rich people had toward the poor. Love for the poor ultimately defined the love of God over Mammon.

PUTTING THE TEXT IN HISTORY: MEANINGS FOR THE WORLD OF AUTHOR-READERS

The story of the rich man and Lazarus spoke directly to Theophilus in layers, starting from the story of the lost son. In the lost son, the story no doubt said much to Theophilus about relationship, in its most intimate terms. Theophilus should treat those who were like the younger son the way he ought to be treated, as an accepted family member. At the very least, the story of the lost son reminded Theophilus that there were some in his life who were like the younger son. He already had relationships with them, at least enough to know that they were bad people.

Here in the rich man and Lazarus story, Luke bluntly pointed out to Theophilus that there were many others to whom he had never planned to relate. The moral argument from the story of the lost son to the rich man parable here moves from lesser to greater demand. In many ways, the story of the rich man and Lazarus proclaimed a more radical message to Theophilus. At least with the lost son, Theophilus had some relationship with the unrighteous. With Lazarus, Theophilus would naturally have treated him as someone invisible. The story forced Theophilus to look actively beyond his immediate circles, to see the invisible people of his society. He would now become a patron to the poor who could give him nothing in return. Instead of amassing wealth, he was to give away his wealth to those he would actively seek. The kingdom value Jesus spoke of would completely upset the system in which Theophilus existed.

MODERN IMPLICATIONS

When looking at the story of the rich man and Lazarus, Luke's logical argument in the entire event speaks well to modern society. If we look at homelessness in modern societies, the problem is alarming. While the social programs of governments solve part of the problem, we still have a long way to go.

Someone remarked to me recently that the church spends a lot of money on big productions of evangelistic and entertainment meetings to attract middle-class "seekers." The common "spiritual" motto people go by would be, "Nothing is too expensive to save souls." However, when someone mentioned that feeding the homeless in the name of Christ would also bring people into the faith, inevitably, many seemingly pious believers would begin to make excuses that the undertaking would be too costly. Obviously, the church has other priorities. Priorities are exactly what Jesus was concerned with.

The godless rich man's life suddenly turned around when he got to Hades. He became quite pious and wanted to help change his family. Abraham spoke to him as if he knew the Law and the Prophets. This is a believer! In other words, the rich man knew that God existed. He was even familiar with the commandments. Similar to the rich man, the Pharisees who sneered at Jesus also knew that God existed and were experts on the commandments. Jesus wasn't saying that all Pharisees were like this. Neither was Luke. However, this group of Pharisees represents a greater problem of people who know better but live as if neither God nor the commandments exist. The rich man living out practical atheism. If this is the culture of the church, it is not too harsh to accuse the church of practical atheism also.

I think our "once saved always saved" doctrine often has trumped the seriousness of Jesus' warnings about future judgment, so much so that we have developed the ability to filter out God's demand. This is quite a serious matter, when professing Jesus' name begins to look like fire insurance. Yet, for many Christians, fire insurance consumes their entire faith. In Luke's usual fashion, this parable speaks against such a single-dimension approach to the gospel. The parable speaks loudly about the resource distribution strategy we take when we prioritize ministry. Where we put our money suggests how we think of eternity. The rich man hardly thought of eternity until it was too late.

Preachers will find a good text in this parable when talking about kingdom stewardship. Yet, we must take care to understand that good stewardship isn't always about money. The broader issue is relationship. Bad stewardship hurts relationships. A preacher shouldn't feel the guilt or burden to preach about money. The sermon should focus on relationship. Yet, this relationship isn't just any relationship, but ultimately relationship with the poor. So, another important issue related to relationship is the Christian treatment of the poor. This may be more challenging, given the diverse views about poverty in the church. Nevertheless, the parable clearly tells us that we shouldn't treat the poor as invisible. While this parable doesn't prescribe a simple solution, it does get people talking about an important issue. The sermon must do the same.

REFLECTION QUESTIONS

1. Why is Lazarus not the main character in the parable?
2. Why is it not helpful to construct what eternity looks like based on this parable?
3. What is the purpose of this parable?
4. How do the stories of the lost son and the shrewd manager help interpret the parable?
5. Why did Jesus talk about divorce in a context where marriage seems irrelevant?
6. How should the church practice the moral of this story?

12

Kingdom Obligations

TELLING IT DIFFERENT: LUKE 17:7-10

> One of you has a slave. One day, the slave came back from the field, and you said to him, "Come at once and sit at the table for a meal after you fix our dinner."

THIS RETELLING OF THE story is probably the most unlikely scenario in Jesus' time. While stories about slaves offend our modern sensibilities, stories about slaves were normal in Jesus' time. A master who did the above would immediately lose his honor in the society. In that slave society, hierarchy was very clear. While a story like the above would fit our modern egalitarian taste, it wouldn't work for Jesus' time. Even a magnanimous master would expect the slave to perform his job.

TELLING IT NORMAL: KEY ELEMENTS IN THE STORY

> 7 Would any one of you say to your slave who comes in from the field after plowing or shepherding sheep, "Come at once and sit down for a meal"? 8 Won't the master instead say to him, "Get my dinner ready, and make yourself ready to serve me while I eat and drink. Then you may eat and drink"? 9 He won't thank the slave because he did what he was told, will he? 10 So you too, when you have done everything you were commanded to do, should say, "We are slaves undeserving of special praise; we have only done what was our duty."

Kingdom Obligations

The passage Luke 17:1–10 serves as the conclusion to the events starting with the journey of Luke 14:25. We shall see that it's an appropriate ending with deep implications. If we look in Matthew 18, we can find a very similar teaching with a very similar moral, but perhaps Luke's teaching is broader. We shall see when we look at the place of this tale in the context of the event starting from Luke 14:25.

We should look at the parable itself here. Jesus used the parable in Luke 17:7–10 to set up a typical scenario in an agrarian society where a slave worked for an owner both in the field and in the house. If this master only had one slave to do both, he must not have been a very wealthy master, but it didn't matter because even a less wealthy master deserved full service. A slave was still a slave whether he worked for a wealthy or less wealthy master. Using this very brief glimpse into a slave society, Jesus showed that servanthood was a given within a hierarchical society. Servanthood under the slave system didn't allow free choices. Luke 17:5 is Luke's first usage of "apostles" since Luke 9:10 to describe the disciples. Luke conceptualized the apostles as servants. Now that we've determined the role of the servant, we should see what servants actually had to do.

In Luke 17:7–10, Jesus set up the equally impossible situation of the owner telling the slave to sit down to eat after a hard day in the field in Luke 17:7b. The most likely scenario would be for the owner to tell the slave to fix supper for the owner to eat first, before the slave would eat in Luke 17:8. Jesus then gave the most unlikely scenario of the owner thanking the slave in Luke 17:9 because, after all, the slave was only doing his duty. To be an apostle, an honorific title to be sure, is to be a slave. Leaders like these apostles were first and foremost slaves. Slaves had no choice other than to do what they were told. We shall see below how all the teachings of obedience tie together with the rest of the context.

CONTEXT

Now is a good time to connect the idea of the obedient slave to the context. At the start in Luke 17:1–3, Jesus shifted focus from the debate with the Pharisees in Luke 16:14–31 to talk about the consequences of causing someone to sin. Jesus compared a painful form of death, drowning, as being preferable to God's judgment on causing a little one to stumble in Luke 17:2. Why were the little ones so hard for the disciples to forgive? It is because such weak little ones would repent and ask for forgiveness through repeated trespasses. Jesus' suggestion in Luke 17:4 was still to forgive, and he seems to equate the little ones with the repentant brother. The commands in Luke 17:3 to rebuke and forgive were directed to the individual offended person in the singular "you" (the Greek "you" has a singular and a plural), emphasizing individual responsibility to practice the commands. Jesus was not saying that the responsibility was not corporate but that the choice had to be individualized. This responsibility went both ways for Jesus' followers, for both the offended and the offender. Here, Jesus was not talking about cheap forgiveness without repentance and rebuke here. The idea that complete reconciliation could happen without confrontation is completely unbiblical. All who are involved need to do their parts. Luke 17:3 clearly says that the erring brother could repent. No one could do the rebuking and forgiving for each individual who had to make that choice to pursue righteousness with love.

Instead of agreeing with Jesus' command to forgive, the apostles asked Jesus to increase their faith in Luke 17:5. Since perhaps forgiving such an annoying person took so much out of them, they thought that forgiveness was a matter of faith. Jesus instead told them the parable in Luke 17:7–10 to show that it was a matter of duty and not of faith. The apostles asked for more faith with the assumption that a certain amount (probably not the size of a mustard seed either) of faith was already present. Of course, the problem the disciples stated was not as impossible as planting a tree in the sea, but that was the way they perceived it. So, Jesus compared the greatness of the perceived problem of the disciples with a realistically impossible problem. If only a tiny bit of faith could solve an impossible problem, then certainly the solution to their problem was not in the amount of their faith. If the task was as great as planting a tree into the sea as the disciples perceived it, such a task only required a faith as small as a mustard seed, which is why Jesus wanted to move their focus from faith to duty, as if to say, "You're going about this in the wrong way. Your problem is not the quantity of faith." The disciples thought that empathizing with and forgiving the weak brother was the maximum expression of discipleship, so much so that they needed gigantic faith, but Jesus used the parable to indirectly rebuke them. By using the slave parable, Jesus said that forgiveness was only a basic duty. The context of the immediate conversation is quite easy to understand. Now, we can look at the broader context of the entire episode from Luke 14:25 to see how this story fits within it.

Kingdom Obligations

From the initial call to discipleship in Luke 14:26, Jesus talked about sacrificing relationship for the kingdom, but what did that look like? It looks something like what Jesus did with the tax collectors and sinners in Luke 15, while risking the disdain of religious leaders. Thus, the call for discipleship focused on sacrificing one kind of relationship, the kind favorable to self, for another kind of relationship, the kind that earned no social favor. This new way of discipleship involved serving God by building relationships and sacrificing money in Luke 16:1–18, an aspect that drew further disdain from the Pharisees in Luke 16:14. This disdain actually encouraged Jesus to teach about the importance of the poor and marginalized in Luke 16:19–31. The theme of being marginalized continues to thread through Luke 17:1–4. The marginalized includes the little one, the weaker brother in Luke 17:1–4.

The disciples still didn't recognize that relationship with the marginalized was what Jesus was talking about repeatedly. This relationship wasn't peripheral to the disciple's social interaction. This embrace of the marginalized was the core value of kingdom relationships. Instead of seeing Jesus' teaching as the basic value of the kingdom, the disciples saw it as one of the highest standards, requiring exceptional faith. Such relationships were a central part of faith and what it meant to take up the cross to follow Jesus in Luke 14:27. To count the cost, like in Luke 14:28, would include moving away from convenient relationships into some of the most inconvenient relationships. We must recall that Luke 14:25 shows that large crowds were chasing Jesus. This set of hard teachings might have thinned the crowd a bit. Jesus was not after numbers. He was after radical commitment and subversive relationships.

If we read the entire story together as one single event from Luke 14:25, we have a story about a new household or new kinship. Vocabulary about kinship starts the story in Luke 14:26, in the statement that people who come to Jesus must prioritize Jesus over kin. Then, somehow the despised sinner became the little "brother" in the lost son story in Luke 15:30, 32, etc. The cross the disciples had to bear, then, was to make undesirable sinners their brothers. The kinship vocabulary adds to household vocabulary of Luke 16–17. Both Lazarus and the rich man called Abraham the father (Luke 16:25, 30). Yet, the disparity between the rich and the poor was a stark contrast, with the rich household excluding the poor. Only one was the true child of Abraham in the eternal abode while the other one didn't end up in a cursed location.

The ordinary earthly household could not express the kingdom, and that's when Jesus switched the parable about household slaves. While the apostles were leaders of the kingdom, evident in their title as apostles in Luke 17:5, they were nothing but ordinary household slaves in Luke 17:7–10. Slaves were also household members, albeit of the lowest rank. The apostles' status dropped from being children to being slaves, simply because they were to obey in the absolute sense. Their servanthood had to do with their acceptance and forgiveness of the marginalized who were also included in the household, evident by the usage of kinship vocabulary in Luke 17:3b. In the new household, Jesus formed new kinship that would turn upside down the patron-client social classes of his society, where the wayward son became close kin, where the privileged became the rejected member of Abraham's household, and where the leader became a slave. The Christ-centered "household of Abraham" became a place of hospitality and empathy rather than self-centered hoarding.

PUTTING THE TEXT IN HISTORY: MEANINGS FOR THE WORLD OF AUTHOR-READERS

Jesus spoke about the household as a metaphor throughout his parables from Luke 14:25—17:10, but for Theophilus, the metaphor was real. He was the head of household. If we are correct in seeing the church setting for Theophilus to be a house church setting, the principles here applied both "in church" and in ordinary everyday life. Theophilus had to run his household through his servants. Yet, he had to become the servant to the less desirable elements of society. His household then became a benevolent location for all kinds of ministries.

In light of what Jesus taught, his management of the household would also change. Instead of lording over those under him, he would identify himself with them in the same way Jesus wanted his followers to identify with the slaves in the parable. This took a great deal of humility and reorientation. If we extend the household situation further into the first-century imperial environment, we can see that Jesus' teaching was very much revolutionary. The household relationships, as I have already stated, were a reflection of how relationships worked in general. The household was the social political glue that kept the society in order. Jesus encouraged his disciples, as Luke encouraged Theophilus, to identify with the weak ones at every turn, and at the same time to not identify with the strong ones, in every parable of this section of the Gospel. In so doing, Jesus had created a new society in Theophilus's sphere of influence. These were the politics of Jesus (and of Luke).

MODERN IMPLICATIONS

Forgiveness is tough. Jesus never denied its toughness. In fact, it's like the tough work of a slave. Forgiveness is like plowing in the field and then having to come home only to fix dinner. Forgiveness is also an obligation rather than a favor to the master. Yet, toughness is part of the duty. Many people see resentment and grudge bearing as something they want to hang onto.

This lesson will weigh heavy on the modern believer's mind because we live in a very broken society where people, even our closest kin, hurt us. There are many cases where we feel that the harm they've done is so irreversible and horrible that we need to hold it over them for a lifetime. This sentiment is very much understandable, especially with sexual abuse victims. Is there a limit to the forgiveness Jesus was talking about?

I think the above question is very difficult to answer pastorally. The biblical view of such trespasses is clearer in Romans 13:4 where the government judges lawbreakers. Jesus' context has to do with a general relational trespass not involving such severe breaking of the law. This is not to say that victims of sexual abuse can't forgive. Surely, they can, and they have, but we have to be quite careful here. The forgiveness Jesus referred to has to do with both sides coming to the table. The offending side is actually the weak one, an erring brother, much like the little ones who need to be protected. This involves repentance and genuine change of heart (Luke 17:4). This also involves discernment about the offenders, as to whether they are the weak ones or not. Not every offender is a weak brother or sister. A priest, a pastor, a teacher or parent can hold immense power over those whom they abuse sexually. Jesus wasn't talking about such cases. The condition for forgiveness must come from repentance on the part of the offending party. The easy forgiveness advocated by many modern pastors, especially in the area of sexual abuse, is inexcusable. Modern believers need to read carefully what Jesus talked about here. Reconciliation needs to come from both sides, and the chief responsibility still lies with the offender rather than the offended.

Preaching this very firm and difficult teaching is risky. I have heard the story of a pastor who made his congregation members imaginatively relive their offense so that they could see their offenders in their minds. This psychological exercise was quite harmful to those who had been severely traumatized. The added guilt from the preacher's careless reading of this passage didn't help. It won't help today either.

The preacher ought to understand that Jesus was talking about a particular kind of relationship first and foremost in which confession, forgiveness and reconciliation are part of this picture. The parable is particularly helpful in that Jesus had asked the disciples to identify with the slave while sympathizing with the weak members of the community. In today's terms, the preacher can ask those who have the power to forgive to identify with the powerless, and see their role to forgive the repentant as not only a choice, but as a duty. This is the suggested route for preaching the passage. A practical suggestion is to devote a good amount of time to talking about the slave parable first, before pointing back at the conditions of forgiveness. But the whole sermon must ultimately arrive at the same place as the whole of Luke 14:25—17:20: God cares about relationships.

REFLECTION QUESTIONS

1. Why did Jesus use a parable about slavery?
2. How is this slavery parable related to forgiveness?
3. What limitations, if any, did Jesus set for forgiveness?
4. How does this story fit within the section of Luke 14:25—17:10?
5. Why did Jesus use household metaphors throughout this event?

13

The Unjust/Lazy Judge and Prayer?

TELLING IT DIFFERENT: LUKE 18:1-8

> In a certain city there was a good judge who feared God and respected people. There was also a widow in that city who kept coming to him and saying, "Give me justice against my adversary." Very quickly, he gave her a just decision because he feared both God and respected people. Won't God give justice to his chosen ones, who cry out to him day and night? Will he delay long to help them? I tell you, he will give them justice speedily.

THE ABOVE WOULD BE an ideal situation where a human judge, in his limited way, can be compared to God. In the days of Jesus, the magistrates such as Gallio would sit on their seats to listen to the complaints of the town and grant judgment based on Roman law (cf. Acts 18:12–17). In fact, we can still see Gallio's judgment seat in old Corinth today. Since the Romans ruled the empire by law, they sought to use the law to bring justice and maintain peace. Certainly, an unjust judge would bring the empire into disrepute, and may have reflected the patron-client relationships he had with the powerful. If the powerful were to oppress the poor (and the unjust judge ran with the powerful circle), then the poor wouldn't get the judgment they deserved. Even if he wasn't dealing with the poor in this case, he was just being plain lazy.

When looking at a scenario above, we have the tension between the ideal and the systemic reality. The system often failed the ideal. The system in fact could potentially work against justice and law. This still happens today in some of the countries that have just laws that never get carried out because of rampant corruption from top to bottom. Even in our imperfect system in the West, this can potentially happen still.

TELLING IT NORMAL: KEY ELEMENTS IN THE STORY

> 1 Then Jesus told them a parable to show them they should always pray and not lose heart. 2 He said, "In a certain city there was a judge who neither feared God nor respected people. 3 There was also a widow in that city who kept coming to him and saying, 'Give me justice against my adversary.' 4 For a while he refused, but later on he said to himself, 'Though I neither fear God nor have regard for people, 5 yet because this widow keeps on bothering me, I will give her justice, or in the end she will wear me out by her unending pleas.'" 6 And the Lord said, "Listen to what the unrighteous judge says! 7 Won't God give justice to his chosen ones, who cry out to him day and night? Will he delay long to help them? 8 I tell you, he will give them justice speedily. Nevertheless, when the Son of Man comes, will he find faith on earth?"

The parable was set in a town with an impious and unjust judge in Luke 18:2. Typical of Luke's concern is the appearance of the poor widow to beg the judge for justice against an oppressor. Luke loved the poor and the marginalized. Obviously any judge that needed a widow to beg to give justice is a bad judge. In fact, whether the widow was poor mattered little, simply because widows were so disadvantaged in their society. For her to get justice was important to prevent her from being abused. Instead of doing his job, he ruled in favor of the oppressor by not doing anything. The ideal judge would look at the case and make a good and fair judgment. To make matters worse, Luke 18:4 says that he refused. Yet, after the repeated annoying pleading, he said to himself in Luke 18:4 that even though he neither feared God nor cared about humans, he had to do something for the annoying widow. Instead of seeing himself as the oppressor, the narcissistic judge saw himself as the victim of the tireless pummeling of the widow in Luke 18:5. To get her off his back, he would seek justice for her. He didn't do it out of his sense of justice or duty; he did it out of annoyance.

If Jesus told the story like the different retelling above, then there would have been every reason to believe that the judge represented God. In fact, some preachers draw the parallel between the unjust judge and God, but Jesus wasn't drawing that parallel. In this case, Jesus drew a contrast.

The Unjust/Lazy Judge and Prayer?

The focal point in Luke 18:4 shows that the judge was godless and selfish. In portraying the inner world of the despicable judge in Luke 18:4, Jesus contrasted the judge with God in Luke 18:7–8. If an unjust judge would help a widow because of annoyance, why would God, who cares about justice and his chosen people, not hear the cry of his people? Thus, the reasons for praying without giving up were two: First, God was much better than the unjust judge. Second, God's people were more precious to God than the widow to the judge. In summary, the reason for not giving up on prayer was because of God's character and God's relationship with his people. So far, the parable and its lesson to the disciples are very straightforward.

CONTEXT

It is so easy to read this parable as a moralistic story about prayer, but it really wasn't just about prayer. It was part of a greater whole coming from an event starting at Luke 17:20, where a Pharisee asked Jesus a question about the coming of the kingdom on the way to Jerusalem (cf. Luke 17:11). Jesus replied in Luke 17:20–21 by explaining what the kingdom was and what it wasn't. Jesus stated these facts as his thesis. First, the kingdom of God could not be observed in terms of locations out there. Second, the kingdom of God was within them.[1] In other words, Jesus was saying that even after careful observation, the Pharisees simply missed the obvious that the kingdom was right in their midst. The presence of Jesus was the sign. They were in the presence of a king and they didn't realize it.

In Jesus' set of teachings, the kingdom came in several forms. First, its coming would be quite sudden or unexpected (Luke 17:22–24, 26–29) but not before his own suffering (Luke 17:25). Second, its coming would result in suffering and judgment of the world (Luke 17:26–29, 30–25). Third, its coming would be as obvious as vultures being near dead bodies (Luke 17:37). If anyone needs to ask, "Is this the day of the Son of Man?" most likely, it is not. If what Jesus said about the cross and suffering came true, then the coming of the Son of Man would also come to pass.

Now, having understood the content of the context, we must return to the parable to see how our understanding ought to impact the interpretation

---

1. The plural "you" in Luke 17:21 didn't mean to have the kingdom in one's heart, per popular interpretation. The plural "you" denotes the crowd following Jesus, including the Pharisees. Due to the fact that the king in God's kingdom (i.e., Jesus) stood before the Pharisees, the kingdom was among them.

of the parable. This parable teaches more than prayer. If we link the teaching about prayer with its final question in Luke 18:8b and the context just prior to the parable, the meaning of the parable expands. In Luke 18:8, Jesus' ending question was important, but unexpected. It only gives significance to the parable if it links back directly to the previous discourse on the day of the Son of Man. This is interesting because the parable seems to talk about quickness in answering the widow, while there was a delay in the coming of the Son of Man. Within the context, the teaching about faith on earth points to a necessary faith in a good God even if the prayer didn't get an answer. The delayed response could well be like the delayed coming of the Son of Man. While the wicked judge didn't have reason for delaying, God sure would have because God is good.

A broader perspective within the teaching of Luke also points to similar truths about answered prayer. We mustn't lose sight of Luke 11:13 where Jesus talked about God giving good things to those who asked, even giving them the Spirit. Luke's teaching on prayer seems to anticipate delayed answers on some issues. In Luke 11, the coming of the Spirit was also delayed. From these sample teachings on prayer, we learn that delay doesn't negate God's goodness. In Luke 18:8, Jesus asked whether he would find faith or faithfulness on earth when he would come.

How would we define faith or faithfulness? Based on the parable, the best way to define the faith or faithfulness was to link back to the character of God and prayer. Prayer then was the expression of faith in a good God who would give the best to his chosen people while they waited on the coming day of the Son of Man. Faithful prayer is an expression of an unshakeable faith. Not giving up prayer but praying faithfully is an expression of belief in the coming day of the Son of Man, even if that day is delayed. Praying comes from a belief that the same God who would vindicate his people on the day of the Son of Man can also benefit them in the present. He would give them what is good for them. Prayer, then, is a discipline that demonstrates hope in a good God whose delay shouldn't cause the disciple to doubt either God's goodness or his ability and willingness to judge quickly and fairly.

The Unjust/Lazy Judge and Prayer?

PUTTING THE TEXT IN HISTORY: MEANINGS FOR THE WORLD OF AUTHOR-READERS

This story spoke into the judicial system to which Theophilus belonged. As a beneficiary and benefactor of this system, he knew all too well the impossibility of perfect justice. In fact, imperfection was everywhere. The unstable political regimes of that time would cause many to lose hope for any lasting peace, let alone justice. Civil strife between emperors had threatened to destabilize the empire. In the midst of such strife, the announcement of the coming Son of Man and the ensuing disasters would only bring greater worries.

In such worrying times, how did the parable address Theophilus? The unjust judge reminded him of a higher role model that didn't do things for profit but for justice. God in this story was the trustworthy character simply because he was far better than the judge. His care for his own people was the primary motive for his answering of their prayer. In the same way, Theophilus had a practical ethical standard to live by in his own administration of justice. Although he worked within a corrupt system, he should do better simply because of the God he believed in.

Another more important topic is prayer as personal piety. For believers of that time, prayer, fasting, and almsgiving were practices of personal piety (cf. Matthew 6:1–18). This practice of piety was very much part of the early believer's lifestyle. Theophilus learned that prayer ought to be a vital expression of faith. People prayed because they believed that God would hear. However, their faith didn't just express a belief in a God who listened to prayers. The faith was much broader. Their faith expressed a belief that the Son of Man would come back. If this faith seemed foolish at the time, Jesus' discourse about his death confirmed that Jesus' promises were true. By the time of Theophilus, Jesus' death had already occurred. That historical event pointed toward other future events for Theophilus. To him, prayer expressed the belief in those future events.

MODERN IMPLICATIONS

The modern worldview normally doesn't have a place for the supernatural. We call that superstition. When we get sick, we don't normally think "demon possession." When we face difficulty, prayer often is our last resort. The reason may be that for some of us, the Christian God is a deistic god.

He's too far away. He exists, but he sure isn't visible. We can't feel him. So, even when we encounter immense difficulty, we pray only as a last resort.

Now, there's nothing wrong with trying to solve problems using the best of our abilities and resources. Yet, this parable is telling in that it does not focus on resources or ability. It speaks of a God who cares about his people. The parable uses relational language. Even though answered prayer may have benefits, prayer is primarily the Christian means to relate to a God who isn't all that far away, but is intimately involved in the lives of believers. Prayer perpetuates a positive cycle. The more believers pray, the more they learn about God's goodness. The more they learn about God's goodness, the more they pray.

Prayer in the context of this parable points beyond getting stuff from God to relationship with God. More importantly, the practice of prayer is the expression of faith toward the bright future Jesus had promised long ago. Jesus talked about prayer in terms of the coming of the Son of Man when God's kingdom comes in its entire glory. Prayer becomes the expression of that belief. Prayer expresses hope. This, among many other reasons, is why Christians need prayer.

Preachers who preach this parable need to take good care not to identify the unjust judge with God. This is an elementary but quite popular mistake. In order to stimulate the audience, the preacher can try taking on the interpretation of that popular mistake first, before correcting that by using the contrast Jesus set out in Luke 18:7–8. Yet, preachers must also take care to expound with illustrations of how prayer expresses a future hope. This hope fits within the context of the discourse. While there's no time in an average Sunday morning service to explain the context in detail, the illustrations for the sermon on the parable can come from stories about hopeful anticipation (e.g., engagement ring, promised gift, etc.). These will help the audience grasp the importance of prayer not merely as practice of piety, but as a theologically significant act.

REFLECTION QUESTIONS

1. Why did Jesus use the unjust judge in the parable when talking about prayer and God?
2. How did the society cause more injustice?
3. In what way was the unjust society a contrast to the kingdom?

The Unjust/Lazy Judge and Prayer?

4. How does the context provide the frame for interpreting this parable?
5. What are some of the essential elements of prayer based on a fuller interpretation of context?
6. How does the story impact a modern believer's life?

14

"Good" Enough?

TELLING IT DIFFERENT: LUKE 18:9-14

> A Pharisee went up to the temple to pray. He stood and prayed about himself like this: "God, I thank you that I am not like other people: extortionists, unrighteous people, adulterers—or even like this tax collector. I fast twice a week; I give a tenth of everything I get."

WHAT THE PHARISEE SAID was probably true, if we cut out the prayer context. The Pharisee certainly wasn't an extortionist. He wasn't unrighteous or adulterous. Certainly, he wasn't a tax collector. Fasting twice a week and giving a tenth of his everything was also part of his lifestyle. By the standard of his day, the Pharisee was a righteous man. If the original listeners heard what he said, they would agree that he fit the perfect picture of a law-abiding, righteous man. There was certainly something commendable about managing one's life based on God's law. The Pharisee of the time also didn't get mixed up in the dirty Roman politics like the Sadducees sometimes did. So, his not being a tax collector only added to his merit of being faithful to his own people. The Pharisee was a good Jew by all accounts. While Jesus told this story dwelling on the goodness of the Pharisee, he didn't stop there. What story was Jesus trying to tell?

TELLING IT NORMAL: KEY ELEMENTS IN THE STORY

> 9 Jesus also told this parable to some who were confident that they were righteous and looked down on everyone else. 10 "Two men

went up to the temple to pray, one a Pharisee and the other a tax collector. 11 The Pharisee stood and prayed about himself like this: 'God, I thank you that I am not like other people: extortionists, unrighteous people, adulterers—or even like this tax collector. 12 I fast twice a week; I give a tenth of everything I get.' 13 The tax collector, however, stood far off and would not even look up to heaven, but beat his breast and said, 'God, be merciful to me, sinner that I am!' 14 I tell you that this man went down to his home justified rather than the Pharisee. For everyone who exalts himself will be humbled, but he who humbles himself will be exalted."

The parable in Luke 18:1–8 talks about prayer as anticipation of God's just character. This parable continues the topic of prayer in light of God's judgment. Jesus compared two men in the parable in Luke 18:10–13 with two opposite attitudes. The first man was a Pharisee. We have to remember that Jesus told this story before the Pharisees who were already present in Luke 17:20. In the usual posture of prayer, especially public prayer, this Pharisee stood up and prayed about himself while giving thanks to God that he didn't commit blatant crimes that were prohibited by the Law. Jesus specifically said that this prayer was "about himself." The Pharisee added in this prayer a denouncement of the tax collector in Luke 18:11, probably seeing the tax collector nearby in Luke 18:13. He then talked about the acts of piety he did in Luke 18:12, such as fasting twice a week (probably Tuesdays and Thursdays) and tithing. Thus, from the prayer, Jesus portrayed a man who was sure of his own righteousness while judging the unrighteousness of others. The problem of course wasn't the Pharisee's confidence in his own righteousness because his good deeds were commendable. The real problem however was his judging attitude toward the tax collector. His good deeds then became the measuring stick against others. While what he said about the tax collector was public knowledge, he wasn't right in presuming the guilt of the tax collector based on stereotype. We shall discuss this later.

In contrast was the tax collector. Why the tax collector and not some other profession? It is because Luke 15:1 already shows the Pharisee's disdain for such a profession. Here in Luke 18:13, the tax collector's reluctance to stand near shows an attitude of fear. The content of his prayer also shows why he had this reluctance. Instead of making a loud pronouncement about his greatness in Luke 18:13, he beat his chest as a sign of contrition while looking down. He merely gave a very short proclamation about himself that he needed God to have mercy on him because he was a sinner in Luke 18:13. In some ways, this also was a prayer about himself and his own sins, but Jesus didn't say that this prayer was about himself because it was not about his righteousness but about his unrighteousness. In contrast to the Pharisee who prayed out of self-sufficiency, the tax collector prayed out of deficiency. The word "sinner" describes a person who missed his mark in his life. He realized his own deficiency before God.

Why did Jesus contrast the Pharisee with the tax collector? The answer is quite simple. Jesus wasn't attacking all Pharisees here. He only took two moral stereotypical extremes to make a point. The Pharisees of Jesus' time were highly religious people who by all accounts were models of righteousness. The tax collector belonged to the other end of the spectrum. For many, this profession by nature made the man a traitor. Thus, the contrast wasn't about Jesus' hatred for the Pharisee as much as about the quality of moral character between the two men. The Pharisee's self-congratulatory prayer about not being a tax collector would surely have received a hearty "Amen!" from the audience. We must notice that Jesus didn't deny the fact that the tax collector was a sinner. In fact, the sign of contrition by the tax collector in the parable confirms Jesus' view. In Luke's writing however, tax collectors were on the way to getting better through their association with Jesus (e.g., Zacchaeus). While Jesus agreed with the Pharisee that the tax collector was an undesirable sinner, the repentance of the tax collector—as it is in the narrative trend of Luke—showed his determination to do better. Some may be tempted to say that the Pharisee actually thought of himself as being sinless. Probably no Pharisee in Jesus' day was ignorant enough to think of himself as being completely without flaws. Being sinless really wasn't the issue for Jesus with the Pharisee in the parable as much as the feeling of being self-righteous toward others who weren't as upright.

Luke 18:14 points to the main issue. After the prayer, both men would go home from the temple but only the tax collector was justified before God. The contrast then was between the one who exalts himself and the one who humbles himself. Quite often, commentators like to emphasize the psychological dimension of the story by saying that God looks at the heart and that the heart is where the problem lies. Jesus didn't talk about the heart. Neither was he a psychologist. He was talking a public action in a religious setting where two men prayed opposite prayers. A more sociological explanation fits the narrative better than a psychological one, based on both the narrative and the background of Jesus' time period. In Jesus' society of honor and shame, where honor mattered and shame destroyed, a person wanted to earn as much honor as possible. Two kinds of honors existed in those days: ascribed and achieved. Ascribed honor came from one's position in life (e.g., the Pharisee in a high place and the tax collector in a low place). Achieved honor came from one's deeds. In the same system, people also received ascribed and achieved shame.

The Pharisee already possessed ascribed honor, but in his prayer, he also had achieved honor from his good deeds. Jesus, in fact, didn't condemn his good deeds. Having both ascribed and achieved honor put him at the pinnacle of society. In the context of the temple, Jesus' parable demonstrated perfectly to his listeners what it meant to gain honor in a religious setting. The problem of the Pharisee's self-sufficiency wasn't merely pride but lust for recognition by stepping on another who had ascribed shame (i.e., the tax collector). He was proud of the crimes he didn't commit and the acts of righteousness he kept. He stood tall in his pious public prayer. At the heart of the tax collector's deficiency was self-degradation. Were the tax collectors in Jesus' day typically repentant? Probably not! If they repented, they wouldn't have continued in their ways and would have changed their lives like Zacchaeus. This tax collector, even as bad as he was, was atypical of tax collectors of his day. This is where Jesus' parable was most subversive for his audience. Shockingly, this tax collector was ashamed of what he couldn't accomplish. Due to the opposite attitude between the two, the results were different.

Originally, the honor-seeking Pharisee expected to be exalted by his own goodness (and Jesus never denied his goodness), but he was not justified, thus negating the original exaltation he had hoped for. On the contrary, the tax collector expected to be beaten down even more due to his deficiency, but he was justified, thus giving him the place of honor the Pharisee originally wanted to attain. In many ways, Jesus was saying that even someone as bad as the tax collector was justified through repentance. The word "justified" in Luke 18:14 is in the Greek passive voice. That means someone was doing the justifying. The question then should be: "Justified by whom?" Certainly, neither the Pharisee nor the tax collector could justify himself. The only person left to justify in the story was the God to whom they prayed. God was the ultimate authority determining who received honor. God justified such self-deprecating people whether they were Pharisees or tax collectors so long as they took on the attitude of the tax collector in the parable.

CONTEXT

The context of this parable is from the broader narrative in Luke 17. I've already discussed the message Jesus proclaimed before in the last chapter. In summary, Jesus warned that the judgment from the day of the Son of Man would come suddenly, obviously, and severely. Jesus then told the parable about the unjust judge and the needy widow to illustrate how God's infinitely great compassion for his people should cause them to pray even more. After Jesus told the parable about prayer, he proceeded to face another group in his audience in Luke 18:9: the self-righteous and disdainful religious types. Here, Jesus continued his theme of prayer. This time, the setting was the temple, the primary religious symbol of Judaism.

How, in fact, would this parable of the Pharisee and tax collector link back with the day of the Son of Man? The day of the Son of Man would be a judgment day. One's legal standing with God would affect not only the kind of present relationship one had with God but also one's judgment on that day. Not only was it important to recognize the Son of Man among them but also to have the right attitude not only in prayer before God but also in public life before others. Assumed righteousness while living in prejudicial judgment against those whom one deemed unrighteous was no way to be justified on the day of the Son of Man. When reading the parable, we mustn't forget the setting to be public and the two characters were practicing in public their pious deed (common among Jews) of prayer. One's life of piety should come from recognition of the great Judge who would exalt the humble and humble the proud. Pride often comes from putting down the inferior. If this parable is a continuation of the last one, then the ethic of public life (including also prayer) is also part of having faith in the right God in Luke 18:8b.

PUTTING THE TEXT IN HISTORY: MEANINGS FOR THE WORLD OF AUTHOR-READERS

Living in an imperial context, Theophilus's public life was important. Living under kingdom principles, he would find the kingdom of God in tension with kingdom of Caesar. Jesus here has shaped the public life of a disciple by the character of the God he worships. Theophilus was used to praying both in his former religion and his present faith. Yet, Luke wanted him to transcend just prayer. He put prayer into God's salvation history for Theophilus so that when Theophilus prayed, both his attitude and his content would match his gospel.

Theophilus, who was probably a patron of a household church, learned from this parable that the societal value of honor and shame wouldn't apply in his new faith community. True honor came from a contrite attitude before God. He was also not to strive for human approval through good deeds. Such striving would be tempting for a man with means. Yet, he must resist with all his might so that he would stand before God in his proper place, while standing within his community. When a patron like him stood at a lowly place, he would become a role model for others who might be tempted to play societal games with societal rules in the Jesus community. The parable warned everyone of the serious consequences of such secular game playing.

MODERN IMPLICATIONS

Someone on the Internet observed that certain athletes were getting endorsement deals despite having never proven themselves, "It's all about selling yourself." That sums up a lot of what's happening in our time. Honor comes from marketing. This the age of Instagram, Facebook, and Twitter, where the right move in social media can make one a star, even if one has never proven himself or herself in any given field whether in academia, the church, or the athletic arena. Our modern ethos of "marketing first and everything else second" looks a lot like this parable. While this parable deals with prayer, it is using prayer to talk about something else. It is using prayer to talk about one's self-perceptions about honor. The assumed honor the Pharisee had through his dissociation with sinners became his downfall. Much of it had to do with his public display to gain further honor. If public display is the primary way we gain honor, it goes against the very ideal of God's kingdom. Its temptation is huge, when becoming a public figure can be as easy as a click on one's iPhone.

The negative side of this social media development is the danger of overexposure. Most people aren't ready to be a public figure whose life would be under the scrutiny of social media. Recent scandals of the church have continued to make the news. The trouble with social media is that the more developed social media is, the harder it is to appear innocent in any scandal. This works against those who occupy positions like the Pharisee. Many religious workers have fallen victim to social media. Jesus' parable here has much to teach us in our church life. With the scrutiny of the world, the more we use the world's system to our advantage, the harder it is when we fall. Jesus' caution about acting more like the tax collector has real application not only before God but also before humans. It's better to be humble than to be humbled.

Collectively, the church can also learn a lot from this parable. We should pay attention to the fact that this is not an anti-Semitic parable against Pharisees, no more than an unconditional praise for all tax collectors. The Pharisee was there to typify those who claim and act on moral high ground against others they deem less worthy than themselves. Moral high ground, to be sure, is very good. Moral high ground, as a tool of harsh judgment against sinners before God, isn't. To whom does the church often look condescendingly? A prophetic posture should always have a huge dose of humility before both humans and God. The faith community's posture shouldn't be a celebration of how right we are or how much better we are than the imaginary straw men we like to beat up. In many instances, and almost inadvertently, our way of life often looks more like the Pharisees than the tax collector in the modern church. Exaltation doesn't only mean to raise oneself up. Exaltation means to raise oneself up based on moral high grounds. The parable teaches us not to do that, but to be humble before the great day of God's judgment prophesied by Jesus in Luke 17. Before the divine throne, no one can boast on moral high ground.

The parable challenges both preacher and audience alike. For modern preachers, their profession often ascribes to them honor and dignity. Even though many mourn the loss of dignity in the pastoral office, the preacher still has a lot of honor. Why else would a bunch of people go every Sunday morning to listen to him or her instead of staying in bed or catching the latest football game? The character of the Pharisee (as a religious leader) would first and foremost challenge the preacher. It's easier to receive applause than to hear constructive criticism. It's even harder to stay humble when one has ascribed honor. The challenge in preaching this parable not only comes from the message but from the lifestyle of the preacher.

While preaching this message, it is easy to just focus on prayer. Surely, we should talk about prayer, as it is still a practice for Christians today as much as it was for Jews in Jesus' day. Yet, the example we must choose to illustrate our sermon ought to go beyond prayer. It should point toward the coming of the Son of Man who will bring judgment. As such, the parable not only serves as an ethical example, but also as a warning. Jesus' conclusion in Luke 18:14 doesn't only apply to prayer, but also applies to life itself. It's worth exploring what it means to be humble in Luke 18:14. The way to discuss humility ought to be within the honor and shame paradigm not only for the first century but, more importantly, for the twenty-first century. Usage of social media is only one example among many (of course, we should take care that we don't exalt ourselves for not abusing social media either).

REFLECTION QUESTIONS

1. What's the danger of seeing the Pharisee as a representative of Judaism?
2. What's the role of the Pharisee in the parable? How about the tax collector?
3. What interpretations can we derive from Jesus' day regarding honor and shame?
4. Why is this story moving beyond only personal pride and humility?
5. How does this story play out in light of the wider event starting in Luke 17:20?
6. What did Jesus mean by "humility?"
7. How does the story apply in the twenty-first century? Give some examples.

15

Getting the Most of Your Minas?

TELLING IT DIFFERENT: LUKE 19:11–27

> A nobleman went to a distant country to receive for himself a kingdom and then return. And he summoned ten of his slaves, gave them ten minas, and said to them, "Do business with these until I come back." But his citizens hated him and sent a delegation after him, saying, "We do not want this man to be king over us!" When he returned after receiving the kingdom, he summoned these slaves to whom he had given the money. He wanted to know how much they had earned by trading. So the first one came before him and said, "Sir, your mina has made ten minas more." And the king said to him, "Well done, good slave! Because you have been faithful in a very small matter, you will have authority over ten cities." Then the second one came and said, "Sir, your mina has made five minas." So the king said to him, "And you are to be over five cities." Then another slave came and said, "Sir, your mina has made another two minas." The king said to him, "You are to be over two cities."

THE STORY ABOUT THE nobleman would be a familiar one with Jesus' audience. In a society where a very small percentage of the population held all of the land and all of the power, those who worked for the elite would value that privilege. This was their only way to gain access to power. Based on what we know about that time, it was often better to work as Caesar's freedman (i.e., a former slave) than to try to be a self-starter. Many of Caesar's freedmen wielded incredible influence. Even a powerful master's slaves who acted as stewards were better off in many ways than the poor freemen.

Once someone was included in the circle of power, whether through servitude or otherwise, he would feel the obligation and responsibility of that privilege. If given money for investment, everyone involved would do their best to help the master make more money. The above story speaks of the way people dealt with being in such a position of stewardship. It is about how people accessed power. The way Jesus told the story, however, speaks of a dire failure in regard to social customs and personal responsibility. We should now turn to the real story Jesus told.

TELLING IT NORMAL: KEY ELEMENTS IN THE STORY

> 11 While the people were listening to these things, Jesus proceeded to tell a parable, because he was near to Jerusalem, and because they thought that the kingdom of God was going to appear immediately. 12 Therefore he said, "A nobleman went to a distant country to receive for himself a kingdom and then return. 13 And he summoned ten of his slaves, gave them ten minas, and said to them, 'Do business with these until I come back.' 14 But his citizens hated him and sent a delegation after him, saying, 'We do not want this man to be king over us!' 15 When he returned after receiving the kingdom, he summoned these slaves to whom he had given the money. He wanted to know how much they had earned by trading. 16 So the first one came before him and said, 'Sir, your mina has made ten minas more.' 17 And the king said to him, 'Well done, good slave! Because you have been faithful in a very small matter, you will have authority over ten cities.' 18 Then the second one came and said, 'Sir, your mina has made five minas.' 19 So the king said to him, 'And you are to be over five cities.' 20 Then another slave came and said, 'Sir, here is your mina that I put away for safekeeping in a piece of cloth. 21 For I was afraid of you, because you are a severe man. You withdraw what you did not deposit and reap what you did not sow.' 22 The king said to him, 'I will judge you by your own words, you wicked slave! So you knew, did you, that I was a severe man, withdrawing what I didn't deposit and reaping what I didn't sow? 23 Why then didn't you put my money in the bank, so that when I returned I could have collected it with interest?' 24 And he said to his attendants, 'Take the mina from him, and give it to the one who has ten.' 25 But they said to him, 'Sir, he has ten minas already!' 26 'I tell you that everyone who has will be given more, but from the one who does not have, even what he has will be taken away. 27 But as for

these enemies of mine who did not want me to be their king, bring them here and slaughter them in front of me!'"

In Jesus' parable, the nobleman had left the ten minas each to the ten slaves in Luke 19:13. As I said above, the slave of a nobleman could sometimes reap great benefit if he played his cards right. The nobleman's mission for this trip was to have himself appointed king, presumably setting the story in a colonial situation, where many kings headed their own fiefdoms under one Caesar. Jesus said that the subjects didn't want him to be king in Luke 19:14 and had decidedly rejected him by sending a delegation to the king at the top (i.e., Caesar).[1]

Before the nobleman left, he gave a substantial sum to each of the slaves (roughly a year's salary or a bit less). The nobleman clearly told them that they had to do something with the money in Luke 19:13, presumably investment. With such a large sum, the slaves were obviously trusted stewards in the nobleman's household. People didn't just leave large sum of money for slaves to handle if the slaves didn't have financial skill. The large sum then implies the ability of the slaves to invest. Whether the people liked the nobleman or not, he came back. On his return, he talked with the slaves about what happened to the money. The first slave whom the master interviewed claimed that he had made ten times the amount in Luke 19:16 and the master gave him ten cities to take charge of in Luke 19:17. The second slaves claimed that he had made five times the amount in Luke 19:18, thus earning him a reward to take charge over five cities in Luke 19:19. We must notice that the master called the first slave a good servant in Luke 19:17, while the second one didn't get the same compliment. Even among faithful slaves, the master praised some more than others. The nobleman didn't care about protecting the slaves' feelings. After all, their feelings were a nonissue because he was now the king.

The final slave confessed that he did nothing other than burying the money in a piece of cloth in Luke 19:20–21. To make matters worse, the final slave claimed that it was out of fear that he did nothing with the money. We must presuppose that he was competent in investing first, lest we think the master was being unreasonable. Surprisingly, the master didn't deny his

---

1. Snodgrass, *Stories with Intent*, 537, notes that a similar event happened upon the death of Herod the Great, where his sons Antipas and Archelaus went to Rome to petition for the title of the "king of the Jews." Some Jews also went to Rome to campaign against Archelaus. There was no historical record of revenge by Archelaus, however.

harshness in Luke 19:22. In fact, the master embraced the slave's description because many masters were harsh in that society.

Before he pronounced judgment, he asserted that the servant had other alternatives in Luke 19:23 such as putting it with some kind of banking body so that he could have lent it out with interest to collect. The punishment was for the minas to be taken away and given to the person with ten cities in Luke 19:24. In the parable, some objected and said that the person with ten minas already had ten minas, implying that he needed no more. The master then said that for everyone who had, more would be given in Luke 19:26. The definition of the one who has appears to do with whether that person had maximally made use of the profit. The man with no profit was left with nothing. What about those who rejected the king? The king simply said that they were to be killed in front of him in Luke 19:27. The king was harsh with his enemies.

The plot has a two-phase judgment. The first phase brought judgment to the three kinds of slaves. The second phase brought judgment to those who hated the king. It's easy to read too much into the killing of the enemies in Luke 19:27. The killing was just part of the picture that fit that culture. Kings killed enemies in those days. Some may choose to allegorize the two phases with one for the believers first and then the other one for unbelievers. The story doesn't need to be an exact scheme of future judgment. Rather, it demonstrates the seriousness of judgment and stewardship. The money had always been the master's and would always be the masters, but those who served him would receive power and reward for dealing well with the money.

CONTEXT

The parable of the minas is the end of a series of events from Luke 18:15—19:9. It's a very long series of teachings. Moreover, it also introduces Jesus' arrival in Jerusalem. It is therefore important to summarize what just happened prior to this parable to get a proper perspective on why Jesus told this parable and why Luke included this parable in describing the event just prior to Jesus' arrival in Jerusalem.

Although the event seems to have started in Luke 18:15, it would actually be better to see the whole event starting in Luke 17:20. The little children episode would be the continuation of the discussion about God's future judgment in the earlier part of Luke 17. The little children would exhibit some of the traits of those whose membership belonged to the kingdom. They also set the standard for hospitality because they were also to be welcomed by true members of the kingdom. In other words, God would include those who were humble enough to receive those who were also lowly and humble.

The next part focuses on the rich ruler. The man asked Jesus what he must do to inherit eternal life and Jesus told him to give up the very advantage he had for the advantage of the disadvantaged and at the same time Jesus used this teaching moment to show that advantages such as wealth were to be an investment in the kingdom, in which the reward would be much greater than the sacrifice. Right after this, Jesus talked about his own impending death in Luke 18:31–34. After all, the disciples who sacrificed now knew that the victorious road to the cross would be difficult.

With sacrifice in mind, Luke portrayed a blind beggar who had shouted for Jesus in Luke 18:35–43 and received his sight. The story was a faith story about the blind man who didn't go back to society but followed Jesus. Ironically, this blind man juxtaposes against the rich man who was unwilling to follow Jesus. The rich man returned to his place. The blind man left his place and indeed his society in order to follow Jesus who was heading to the cross. While it was hard for the rich man to follow Jesus, it was quite easy for the poor blind beggar to follow Jesus because the rich man perceived that Jesus did nothing for him while the blind man received his sight from Jesus.

Just in case people thought that Luke hated the rich, he stuck a story of the rich follower in Luke 19:1–10. The story portrays Zacchaeus, a man hated by the religious leaders and many Jews because of his profession as not only a tax collector but a "chief" tax collector (cf. Luke 15:1; 19:7) who, instead of settling easily back into his wealth like the rich ruler of Luke 18, gave just about everything he had either to the poor or toward reparations for his victims. This story climaxed with Jesus' comment that Zacchaeus was indeed one of Abraham's children. Luke's message is very simple: if a rich man wanted to be a disciple, he had to use his riches for the right purpose, mostly by getting rid of it. It wasn't impossible. It was just difficult. It was interesting that Jesus talked about salvation being in Zacchaeus's household. What was he being saved from? Clearly, according to the wider context of Luke 17, he was being saved from God's future judgment when the Son of Man would arrive. While people were listening to what Jesus said about Zacchaeus's household, he told them the parable of the minas.

Sometimes, when reading a parable, we wonder whether aspects of the parable contain literal meanings. In this case, there are indeed some literal aspects regarding finances.

When reading the story in light of the social situation of the entire event, we can't help seeing the theme about money cropping up over and over again, along with social class. Thus, the investment of the minas in the parable could be realistically related to how kingdom disciples would treat others with their finances and social advantages. They were to be more like Zacchaeus and less like the rich ruler. They ought to lower themselves like the young children Jesus used to analogize kingdom citizens so that they would be able to benefit the people at the fringe like the poor blind beggar. The context surrounding the parable shows money to be a very important issue. In this case, money wasn't merely a symbol of what one did with the kingdom message. It was rather a symbol of all resources that could be invested in people's lives. The investment didn't need people to have financial sophistication as much as a willing heart to give money away.

There's yet another aspect of this parable that fits the next episode. Jesus was coming to Jerusalem. The king was returning. He returned as a peasant, not with his throng of army but in peace. He was not a rich man, as people expected. Would people accept him? The parable served to warn listeners that acceptance of the coming king and his kingdom was a must. In such a case, the acceptance wasn't something general but something demonstrated quite specifically by how one invested possessions for the kingdom. Those who listened to his radical message, especially his message of justice, would be judged according to their responses much like those three slaves. Those who outright hated him and rejected him would in turn face divine judgment. We must also remember not to read the parable as an anti-Semitic story. It wasn't a parable against Israel, per se. It was a parable against all those who have heard and read Jesus' teaching but continue to ignore the lessons taught, especially regarding helping the poor and living justly.

PUTTING THE TEXT IN HISTORY: MEANINGS FOR THE WORLD OF AUTHOR-READERS

The minas parable spoke strongly to Theophilus. In a society where masters ruled with an iron fist, Theophilus understood authority. He also understood from the parable what it meant to be a slave. Jesus urged his listeners to identify with the slaves who were the stewards of the master's money.

To oppose such a powerful master was unthinkable. Thus, there was no outright opposition to the master by his own slaves.

Theophilus would understand that the possessions he had rightly belonged to the master. Before he became a disciple of the faith community, Theophilus had freedom to do what he wanted with his money. However, now he realized that all that he had belonged to the master. He was only the steward of his possessions. His only option was to invest such possessions for the master. Being a good patron was not enough. He needed to give in a way that wouldn't expect returns. This would create a radical shift in the way he would deal with his position of power.

Theophilus would also see that the master in the parable had enemies. Who were the enemies? Those were the ones who didn't buy into the kingdom value system. Some of these enemies eventually killed Jesus. Lest we think that Luke was spouting anti-Semitic stories, the story wasn't mainly against the Jews. The story mainly depicted opposing value systems. Those who didn't buy into the value system of Jesus would oppose him. Theophilus, through this story, realized that there's no neutrality when it came to kingdom values. He was either for or against that value. Those who were against were capable of great harm. That's why they would be judged in the coming of the Son of Man.

MODERN IMPLICATIONS

Recently, Mark Wahlberg, the famous actor, asked for a pardon for a hate crime he committed years ago as a kid. I enjoy a lot of Wahlberg's movies, and unlike many who really dislike his action, I'm not about to boycott all his movies, but his case does bring up an interesting ethical problem.

Reactions have included the extremes of either saying that Wahlberg doesn't deserve any pardon or that he deserves a second chance. Then, there are the reactions in between. According to Wahlberg, he said that he has paid back society by doing good deeds in the form of charities. According to the Asian American man who lost his eye in the racist attack, he has pardoned Wahlberg, and says he ought to be commended for his generosity. Yet he also states that Wahlberg has never reached out to him. The lack of real reconciliation causes one of Wahlberg's other victims to call for no pardon. Why not let bygones be bygones?

The answer is very simple. Good works do not always lead to reconciliation. They never replace reconciliation. Every sin or crime against real victims demands reparation for the victims. Unless the perpetrator reaches out and makes reparation to victims, good works can't hide past sins, and they certainly do not redeem the sinner. Rather, good works distract from the real issue of reparation. Wahlberg is sidestepping the issue. Feeling sorry and doing "some" good works aren't the answer to the problem. If Wahlberg wants good will, perhaps taking financial steps to make reparations to his victims is the best way to earn some good will. Start with, "I'm sorry for your eye. Here's a few million dollars from my stash of several other millions." Just prior to the parable, Zacchaeus's story illustrated such an approach, and the parable only confirmed the need for this kind of action. The parable Jesus told doesn't allow easy escape and cheap grace for believers. If anything, it demands a greater accountability in one's relationship with others.

In the same way as stated above, Christians who behaved badly before their conversions often hide behind their present new lives, as if God's grace is somehow a justification for their past wrongs. We're living in the real world with real victims. If Christians are truly justified, then they ought to understand that justification should result in justice. The justified should value justice more, not less. Free grace is not cheap. A changed life isn't the same thing as reparation or real reconciliation. A changed life isn't just about feeling sorry for messing up. A new life demands action that brings forth reparation, reconciliation, and hospitality toward others.

It is easy to preach the parable of the minas like the parable of the talents in Matthew 25:14–30. As we may recall, the section of Matthew 25:14–30 is part of the greater discourse about the temple. The talents parable in Matthew 25 very likely criticized some of the problems created by the temple.[2] At the same time, the talents parable encouraged the disciples to fulfill their duties as members of Israel where the original temple failed. It's a mistake to use Matthew to interpret Luke because Luke's emphasis was so utterly different. Luke's own voice from the context going as far back as Luke 17:20 decides the meaning of the parable. At the end, Jesus was talking about using resources to help others while repairing broken relationships.

A sermon about the minas should focus on several aspects. At the application level, it's best to use examples about helping others or repairing relationships. At the theological level, it's important to keep in mind the grave tone about God's judgment. The judgment includes both reward and punishment. This sermon will challenge any believer who has abundant

---

2. See Tsang, *Right Kingdom*, 120–27.

resources. It will also challenge churches with abundant resources. It should ultimately talk about what God expects. God expects the believer to use resources for restoration of relationship.

REFLECTION QUESTIONS

1. How did working for a nobleman give a slave benefit?
2. What did the owner expect of his slaves?
3. Why was slavery an important analogy for Jesus' time?
4. How did the previous context illuminate the present parable?
5. How did this parable fit with the event that followed?
6. Why is it a bad idea to read Matthew 25 into this parable? What are the differences?

16

Bad Tenants and the Innocent Son?

TELLING IT DIFFERENT: LUKE 20:9–19

> A man planted a vineyard, leased it to tenant farmers, and went on a journey for a long time. When harvest time came, he sent a slave to the tenants so that they would give him his portion of the crop. The tenant farmers paid up, and both the owner and the farmers got their fair shares.

IN JESUS' SOCIETY, TENANT farming was a regular part of the lifestyle. A very small minority of the population owned the vast majority of the land. Due to this disparity between land ownership and labor, the owner and laborers had to depend on one another. The labor force was partly composed of tenant farmers who traded labor for some agricultural products and living quarters. The other parts of the labor force could also be slaves who were hired by either the landowners or the tenant farmers. This system required cooperation from both sides. Sometimes, it favored the owner, but often, it required both sides to give a little. After all, if the owner were known to be scam artist, the tenant farmers would know better than to work for him and would choose other owners with greater sense of fairness. The above short story would typify such a harmonious relationship between the haves and have-nots. Jesus didn't tell his story in this way. In fact, he told a very turbulent story that was bound to upset more than a few of his listeners.

Right Parables, Wrong Perspectives

TELLING IT NORMAL: KEY ELEMENTS IN THE STORY

> 9 Then he began to tell the people this parable: "A man planted a vineyard, leased it to tenant farmers, and went on a journey for a long time. 10 When harvest time came, he sent a slave to the tenants so that they would give him his portion of the crop. However, the tenants beat his slave and sent him away empty-handed. 11 So he sent another slave. They beat this one too, treated him outrageously, and sent him away empty-handed. 12 So he sent still a third. They even wounded this one, and threw him out. 13 Then the owner of the vineyard said, 'What should I do? I will send my one dear son; perhaps they will respect him.' 14 But when the tenants saw him, they said to one another, 'This is the heir; let's kill him so the inheritance will be ours!' 15 So they threw him out of the vineyard and killed him. What then will the owner of the vineyard do to them? 16 He will come and destroy those tenants and give the vineyard to others." When the people heard this, they said, "May this never happen!" 17 But Jesus looked straight at them and said, "Then what is the meaning of that which is written: *'The stone the builders rejected has become the cornerstone'*? 18 Everyone who falls on this stone will be broken to pieces, and the one on whom it falls will be crushed." 19 Then the experts in the law and the chief priests wanted to arrest him that very hour, because they realized he had told this parable against them. But they were afraid of the people.

The parable was an answer to what went on before. More discussions will follow below. For now, Jesus told a parable in Luke 20:9–18 that also has a parallel in Mark 12:1–12 and Matthew 21:33–46.

The original problem had to do with stewardship given by a vineyard owner to some tenant farmers in Luke 20:9. Let me restate the problem already told in the alternate retelling of the story. Quite reasonably, when giving land to tenant farmers and fields to till, the owner expected to collect his share of the harvest in Luke 20:10. The farmers weren't to violate the agreement to give a certain amount of the harvest to the owner. In that time, many rich landowners had their own militias. Violation of their agreement would result in swift and violent punishment.

The first servant that was sent to collect a share of the harvest was beaten up with nothing given to the owner in Luke 20:10. The second servant wasn't just beaten but treated shamefully in Luke 20:11. What shameful treatment they gave him, we do not know. The third servant was beaten up and was injured and ejected in Luke 20:12. Most likely, the parable tells a

Bad Tenants and the Innocent Son?

variation of the same treatment for all three servants. In a society that honored the privileged, the owner thought that sending his son would do the trick in Luke 20:13. Here, the son's rank surely would mean something to these otherwise ruthless tenant farmers. No one would dare to touch him.

In a perfect world, the farmers wouldn't dare to disrespect the son because if they did, violent consequences might follow. Yet, as they saw the coming heir in Luke 20:14, they decided that killing the son would allow them to take over the owner's property. This was a serious matter because the owner said that this son was his beloved son in Luke 20:13. These lawless and fearless tenant farmers took the son out and killed him. The net result of this awful event was that the owner brought his militia in and killed all the murderers. The owner would then bring in other farmers to do this work. The complete violation of social conventions had Jesus' audience saying that this should never be, in Luke 20:16. The expression of the audience in Luke 20:16 is a strong denouncement filled with repulsion (cf. Galatians 2:17, which uses the same expression).

Jesus then told the parable as an explanation by citing Psalm 118:22 in Luke 20:17. Psalm 118 is the ending of the "Hallel Psalms," Psalms 113–118, that would be sung for the Passover season. It was fitting to cite this psalm for this season and this parable. Why would a traditional Passover psalm be great for this occasion? Was it not because the Jewish people wanted to see a complete salvation from God that would resemble their deliverance from oppression in Egypt? The psalm talks about God's faithfulness in restoring Israel. The restoration would involve the righteous being rejected by others but honored by God. That righteous person would be compared to a throwaway stone in a building project. Yet, Jesus brought out the implications of the eschatological judgment of God in Luke 20:18. He claimed that the person on whom the stone fell would be crushed. It is easy to read the temple into the architectural symbolism but that isn't necessarily the only way to read it. The architectural imagery merely illustrates rejection. There's no reason to allegorize any anti-temple rhetoric into the psalm. The important part of all this has to do with rejection. All those who rejected Jesus, whether Jews or Gentiles, would be like the one who stumbled over the rejected righteous man. None of this would end well.

The best way to look at Psalm 118 is to link it to the earlier citation in Luke 13:35 by Jesus with reference to his triumphal entry. Originally, in Luke 13:35, Jesus quoted Psalm 118:26. The quotation blessed the person who would come in the name of the Lord, presumably Jesus in his messianic office. The expectation of course was a blessing rather than judgment. In the quotation of Psalm 118:22 here, judgment was the result in the form of someone falling down on the stone. In the discussion of the parable, the only people crushed were the murderous farmers. The stone that crushed them was the judgment of the landowner.

Some may choose to read the parable as a completely symbolic allegory, with the landowner being God, the vineyard being Israel, the son being Jesus, the tenant farmers being the religious leaders, and the slaves being the prophets. The killing of the servants by the owner via his own militia would typify the killing of the religious leaders by God through his angels. Israel the vineyard didn't belong to the religious leaders. It belonged to God. Perhaps a minimalist approach would give a less symbolic reading. Maybe Jesus was merely saying that the unfaithfulness of the farmers would be unthinkable in his own society. How much more unthinkable would it be for the religious leaders to persecute a true prophet of God like Jesus? Perhaps Jesus was making a simple argument. Certainly, at the very least, Jesus' audience was so repulsed by such a story, that they denounced it in Luke 20:16b.

CONTEXT

The real context that caused Jesus to tell this story came from the events in Luke 20:1–8. The characters involved in this controversy were the religious leaders. The group of leaders in Luke 20:1 receives attention because they represented the power structure of the temple, and we have a story of power struggle between the established power structure and Jesus. While many religious leaders opposed Jesus and some were friendly to Jesus, there weren't groups more representative of the established religious order than the chief priests and the experts of the law. Their main question to Jesus came in two forms in Luke 20:2, "By what authority are you doing these things? Or who is it who gave you this authority?"

Jesus didn't seem to think of these questions as friendly. So, he responded by quizzing them with questions that put them in a socially awkward situation. In Luke 20:3, Jesus asked them whether they believed that John's baptism was from heaven or from humans. In framing his question this way, Jesus basically presupposed that one couldn't have a positive opinion of John (e.g., Josephus) without an equally or even more positive opinion of Jesus himself. The religious leaders knew that. So did Jesus. At the same time, if we think of the parable as suggesting an alternative version where the tenant farmers accepted the demand of the owner, then the rejection of either John or Jesus was not normal. Of all people, the religious leaders ought to have found John and Jesus acceptable.

Jesus was obviously not trying to get an answer from them in his question because the answer throughout Jesus' ministry and Luke's Gospel had been clear: John the Baptist was from God in the same way that Jesus was also from God. Those assumptions about the divine origins of both John and Jesus were already well grounded in the narrative of the Gospel. The leaders discussed the question among themselves in Luke 20:5–6 because they were conflicted between what they believed and what the crowd believed. Their line of thinking indicates that they had never believed in John, let alone Jesus. They also worried that if they said that John's baptism was from humans in Luke 20:6, the people who liked John might endanger them. The answer to the question depended entirely on pragmatism rather than truth. The mention of stoning in Luke 20:6 shows that this could become an issue of orthodoxy because people would stone false prophets and heretics. This parable obviously offended the religious leaders because Jesus spoke the parable against them in Luke 20:19. The audience being "the people" in Luke 20:9 makes this parable something Jesus used both to both talk about, and to condemn, the religious leaders.

The context of opposition sheds light on the parable. The elements between the conflict story and the parable find many connection points. The ironic mention of stoning and the stumbling stone shows that although they were afraid of being stoned by the people, the religious leaders had essentially stumbled on the truth that was set in stone, that Jesus was from God. The pragmatic approach of the religious leaders also reflects well how the tenant farmers dealt with their owner. They calculated that they would be safe and that if the son died, they would take over the entire farm. Their miscalculation resulted in their downfall. In the same way, the miscalculation of the religious leaders would lead to their eventual downfall. Just like the tenant farmers shouldn't have violated their social conventions, neither should the religious leaders violate their own religion.

The conclusion of the story also informs our interpretation of the parable. In the context of Luke 20:19, Jesus exposed those who had murderous intent using the parable, but he wasn't just making a prophetic prediction. He was making a pronouncement of judgment. These leaders would be the ones who rejected the righteous like those who faced judgment in the psalm. If the discussion from Psalm 118 points to Israel's restoration, Jesus was saying that Israel would be restored in spite of the bad elements among some of its religious leaders. Yet, God would judge those leaders, if they rejected Jesus. In saying so, Jesus was also showing that God's work in Israel was not yet done. At this point, at least the people were on the side of Jesus in Luke 20:19, but the religious leaders weren't fond of what Jesus had said, knowing Jesus had spoken this parable against them.

PUTTING THE TEXT IN HISTORY: MEANINGS FOR THE WORLD OF AUTHOR-READERS

For this text to mean something to Theophilus, it has to link back to the history of the reader. Luke wrote this story after 70 CE. It was a time when people would ask about the next step of God's work, now that temple had been demolished by Rome. Luke wanted to point to the importance of Jesus in his position as God's prophet. While the rejection of Jesus was in the historical past, the impact remained within some corners of Judaism. As a person who was connected somewhat to Judaism—a point I've elaborated on earlier—Theophilus needed to know the core of his faith. Jesus was the core of his faith. He mustn't prioritize other things. In his faith community, Theophilus probably celebrated the Christian Passover, the Lord's Supper, quite frequently. The Psalm quotation reminded Theophilus of the importance of Jesus in the midst of any celebration related to the Passover. The theological implication is that the Passover for followers of Jesus had to involve Jesus.

While this story could be used anti-Semitically, it opened up the conversation in a different way for Theophilus. In this period of history, the second half of first century, anti-Semitism was indeed on the rise. But this wasn't an anti-Semitic story. Neither was it a story denouncing rituals in the temple. Rather, it was a story about the how Jesus fit into God's greater plan for Israel's history, a plan that included Passover symbolisms. The quotation of Psalms 113–118 demonstrated this for Theophilus.

Rather than turning to an anti-Semitic focus, Theophilus might see the point of this story to be related to leadership. The portrait of these negative leaders would inform Theophilus about what true leadership should be. The leadership that opposed Jesus in the story didn't just reject Jesus but their conviction also changed, based on the wind direction of popular opinions. They were afraid to speak from their own convictions because of the crowd. The portrait speaks more about their character than merely the truth they believed in. Theophilus would learn a lesson about leadership in a faith community. In direct contrast, Jesus who would eventually go to the cross would be killed for showing forth the kingdom.

MODERN IMPLICATIONS

The parable has modern implications. Obviously, one implication is related to salvation and Jesus. Besides the obvious, the implications for leadership are huge. The way the tenant farmers handled their stewardship reflects on the leadership that opposed Jesus. How in fact did they oppose Jesus? They simply used their power to spy out Jesus' work in order to advance their cause. To make matters worse, they also kept silent about what they believed because of the crowd. Thus, they reflected their own ethics both actively and passively. Actively, they tried to figure out ways to murder Jesus. Passively, they kept quiet about what they believed to be true simply because of the popularity of Jesus. Their silence wasn't in order to be polite. Their silence was deadly because the occasion was not right to murder Jesus.

While we definitely shouldn't think that all the religious leaders in Jesus' day were evil, we must notice the portrait of evil leadership here being sharply applicable to modern faith communities. The politics of faith communities can intertwine with the interests of its leaders and vice versa. Politics can be the greatest enemy of truth because truth often upsets the status quo. The politics of silence can hurt a faith community. The politics of devious plotting also murders truth. This story ought to inform both the faith community and its leaders. Self-interest will destroy integrity.

Preaching this parable is a straightforward affair. The plot is simple. The parable has two sides, the normal side, representing the expected social conventions, and the side that Jesus told. The preacher must be aware of the normal side in presenting the material so that the audience can get the unusual circumstances of the way Jesus told the parable. In so doing, the preacher should link the parable to the religious leaders who rejected Jesus. The contextualization must point at the way leadership is done today, rather than pointing a judgmental finger at those religious leaders. The audience must know that it's easier to judge ancient religious leaders than our own religious communities that are often fraught with the same forms of stumbling as we find in Luke 20.

REFLECTION QUESTIONS

1. What advantages and disadvantages are there for reading the parable as an allegory?
2. What were the normal circumstances by which the tenant farmers should have operated?
3. Why was Jesus' audience so appalled?
4. What does the parable have to do with the religious authorities' questioning of Jesus?
5. How is Psalm 118 significant in both the parable and in Luke's Gospel?
6. What were the main problems exemplified by the religious leaders?

Bibliography

Ferguson, Everett. *Backgrounds of Early Christianity*. Grand Rapids: Eerdmans, 1993.
Levine, Amy-Jill. *Short Stories by Jesus*. San Francisco: Harper, 2014.
Malarkey, Kevin, and Alex Malarkey. *The Boy Who Came Back from Heaven*. New York: Tyndale, 2010.
Snodgrass, Klyne. *Stories with Intent*. Grand Rapids: Eerdmans, 2008.
Tsang, Sam. *Right Kingdom, Wrong Stories*. Eugene, OR: Wipf & Stock, 2013.
———. *Right Texts, Wrong Meanings*. Eugene, OR: Wipf & Stock, 2013.

www.ingramcontent.com/pod-product-compliance
Lightning Source LLC
Chambersburg PA
CBHW051939160426
43198CB00013B/2226